The End™

The Boston Massacre

THE CHRONICLES OF SURVIVAL AFTER THE END OF CIVILIZATION...

Eloi, Eloi lama sabachthani?
My God, my God, why hast thou forsaken me?
Matthew 27:46

A Supplement for the Roleplaying Game of the Biblical Apocalypse brought to you by

Tyranny Games

Written by
Derek Guder and
Joseph Tierney

Written By:

Derek Guder

Joseph Tierney

System Design:

Joseph Tierney

Martin Tierney

Jeff Konkol

Editing:

Joseph Tierney

Martin Tierney

Art Direction:

Joseph Tierney

Martin Tierney

Typesetting and Layout:

Martin Tierney

Artists:

Unheilig

Martin Tierney

Michael Everett

Matt Thompson

V. Shane

SPECIAL THANKS:

Thank you to the families and friends of all involved.

A very special episode of Thanks to:

Jurgen "Giant Clam of the Apocalypse" Meyer for... well... Machiavellian Shellfish of Doom. What else? The good Mr. Jason Blair, for the introduction that got it all started. Alex Jurkat and George Vasilakos at Eden Studios for employing Mr. Guder. The door to it all was opened by Sandy Antunes and the establishment of RPGnet. And finally, the Other Derek (Stoelting, that is).

DISCLAIMERS:

The End - The Boston Massacre is a work of fiction. Any similarity between characters and events portrayed in this book and any real persons, living or dead is purely coincidental and wishful thinking on behalf of some lawsuit-hungry party.

The premise of *The End* is based on Judeo-Christian apocalypse stories. This does not represent a religious statement on behalf of the management of Tyranny Games LLC, nor is it meant as a religious treatise. It is just a game, folks.

This is only a game. If, at any time, what happens while playing *The End* becomes more important than reality, seek competent psychiatric help.

Due to the subject matter of *The End*, this product should be used only by those individuals mature enough to handle it. We recommend a minimum age of 17 be required before playing.

All Biblical quotes as well as chapter and verse notations come form the King James version of the Bible, available everywhere.

Contents

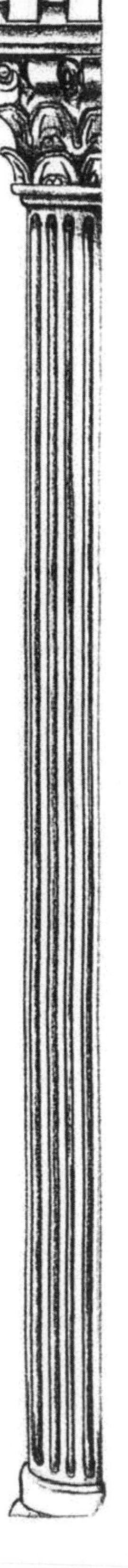

unHeilig

Chapter One

Introduction

Intent and Use

The Boston Massacre is a self-contained adventure and sourcebook built on the violent struggles facing the small colony of survivors who have laid claim to Boston in the world of ***The End***. It is not, however, a story with a final conclusion. The trials that Boston and her "Sons of Liberty" face cannot be resolved within the space of a single adventure. The rise and fall of a colony takes much longer. Neither success nor defeat is so easy.

Furthermore, this adventure serves as a starting point for future events on the East Coast. There is a terror lurking in Washington, D.C., and it hungers for Boston. If that proud and desperate colony falls, it is unlikely that D.C.'s dark appetite will be sated. With the thorn of Boston removed from its side, that evil will be able to turn its attention to the other colonies that have managed to rebuild themselves after the Rapture. If Boston cannot hold on to its hard-won survival, can the other colonies?

With this in mind, *The Boston Massacre* has been written so that the immediate events contained within it are brought together and closed by the end, but threads are left open for continuation. This adventure is not meant to be an entire campaign or chronicle itself, but a piece of one, perhaps even the very beginning of a campaign.

A Break-Down of the Chapters

The section you are reading right now, **Chapter One: Introduction**, is just that, an introduction. It is meant to give you a clear idea about what this entire book is for, as well as what it contains. As such, it contains not only enough setting information on New England to give the adventure some context, but also a brief summary to help the Judge have a solid grasp of the material presented.

Chapter Two: the Boston Metropolitan Area serves as a very brief tour of Boston, just enough to provide the Judge with the material needed to invent their own Boston in the world of ***The End***. This chapter also provides all of the information on major residents of the city in a central location, for ease of reference during play. The states of Rhode Island, Connecticut and Massachusetts are explored in **Chapter Three: Southern New England** while **Chapter Three: Northern New England** looks at New Hampshire, Vermont and Maine. The characters and locations presented therein provide Judges with fodder with which to create further adventures.

Chapter Four: Act I is the opening act of the adventure, where everything begins and the players are introduced to the colony of Boston and most of the major players of this drama. Following that is **Act II**, in which conflict and excitement are brought to the fore to get the blood pumping and keep the players involved in the story. **Act III** takes a pause from that excitement to provide the opportunity for the players to mull over the events they have experienced and piece things together, but that is

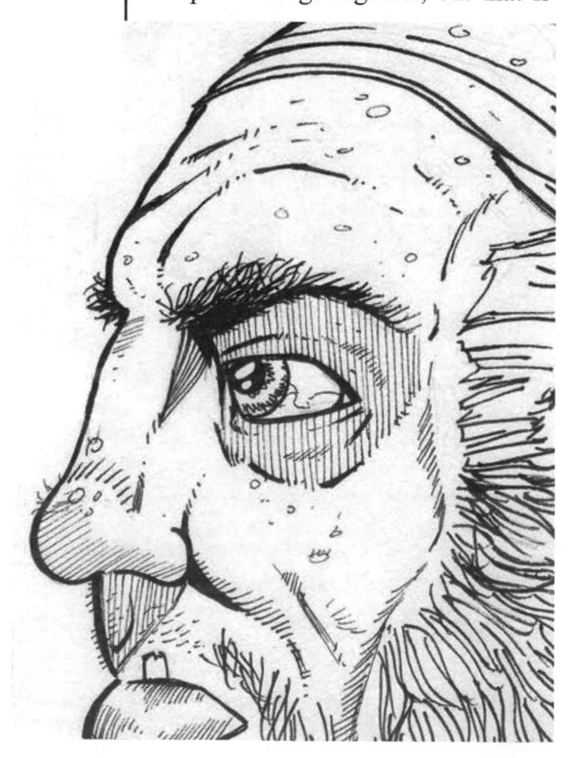

not to say it is without its surprises. Finally, **Act IV** concludes the adventure, giving the players the opportunity to shape the destiny of the Boston colony. **Appendix A: Judges Advice,** notes and explanations provides a wealth of advice and resources for Judges looking to expand, change or alter the events of *The Boston Massacre*. **Appendix B: Founder Reborn Class** details the new Founder Reborn (Prestige) Class. **Appendix C: Non-Player Characters and Creatures** details the NPCs and creatures for the adventure.

A Brief Summary

Boston welcomes a number of ragged refugees (Slang: "Refuse") just before a mysterious enemy launches another series of attacks against them- apparently designed to gauge the colony's strength. Boston responds with its own scouting mission, which leads the Sons of Liberty (slang: "SOLs") to believe the army ultimately hails from Washington, D.C. Given little time to prepare, the Sons of Liberty attempt to defend their colony from the invaders as best they can, but their cause seems hopeless until the enemy mysteriously and miraculously withdraws. Lt. Col. Jefferson takes the opportunity to send out a number of long-distance foraging parties in an attempt to replace supplies lost in the fighting, and in the hope of finding another colony to form an alliance.

The players should be recruited as one of these foraging parties. While on this scavenging mission, the players discover the truth behind an unknown disease that made its first appearance in the colony shortly after the refugees arrived. Before they race back to Boston to avert a tragedy, they also discover the supplies the colony so desperately needs, as well as evidence of another colony they may be able to enlist help from. Upon returning to Boston, fighting through somewhat unnerving and supernatural resistance, they are embroiled in a power struggle within Boston, centered on which course of action to take regarding the refugees.

Depending on their actions, the players may avert or cause a massacre and on the longer term they may save or fail the entire colony of Boston.

A Word to the Judges

This is not a pretty adventure, nor is it a very nice one. This story deals with tough choices and forces the players to make a decision that not everyone may be comfortable with. It is entitled *The Boston Massacre* for a reason, because that is what it can very easily become depending on how events unfold. Do not take this lightly.

Keep the tastes and boundaries of your players in mind when running this game. Your players may get uncomfortable if you provide too much detail on the trials the refugees faced during their flight from New York or what happens when the disease ravages them. Don't provide intricate details of the violence if you know or even suspect that it will make your players uncomfortable.

Scope

The events of this story are largely centered on the remains of the city of Boston, although **Act III** involves an extended trip into western Massachusetts and Connecticut. This keeps the physical scope of the game manageably small. It is a good idea to keep a tight control on the scope of the game as it progresses, and let it slowly widen as the story unfolds, until it reaches the desired expanse.

Theme

The theme of *The Boston Massacre* is that life will sometimes demand tough choices, and sometimes people are faced with a choice between two evils. Either decision, in the end, demands responsibility and acceptance of the consequences. Sometimes running from those consequences and "deciding" to make no choice at all will only make things worse.

Life isn't easy, and life for the Meek is even harder. Not only is survival a daily struggle now, but God has turned his back on them. There is no longer anyone else to turn to for answers, no undeniably higher power in which people can place their trust and feel comfort in knowing that they are doing the right thing. The only thing a man can rely upon now is himself, and he is the only one who can say whether he has done right or wrong. Is mankind ready for that responsibility? This adventure explores that question.

The Real World

Judges may or may not want to refer to real world maps and documents to provide detail and realism to this adventure. We have also provided some maps. On the whole, *The Boston Massacre* provides enough details to ground itself and provide a starting place for Judges who do want to research more detail. Groups comfortable with a much more loose gaming style needn't worry, as setting the game against a much less distinct backdrop of streets and forests is just as easy.

Mood

The Boston Massacre goes through a variety of moods. Each act has its own distinct atmosphere and feel. The mood of the adventure taken as a whole, however, is one of survival. Boston is embroiled in a war, and it doesn't look like it is going to get better any time soon. The colony is doing its best to survive while remaining true to the ideals of the nation whose ashes it rose from. Caught in the jaws of the war, it may very well find out that the strong survive, not the idealistic.

Pacing

Just as the mood of the adventure varies wildly during its length, so too does the pacing. Like the scope, the Judge should keep a close eye and a tight reign on how events unfold. Roughly, **Acts I** and **III** have slow paces. They are periods of introduction, reflection and comprehension. **Acts II** and **IV**, on the other hand, have much faster and more hectic paces. Conflict and action define **Acts II** and **IV** and things should happen fast enough to engender that feeling. Each chapter has a more detailed look at pacing considerations.

Experience

Experience should be awarded not only for combat or defeated foes but for completion and survival of situations as the party moves on. Survival of each act should be equivalent to defeating a CR 5 opponent and Judges should be aware of bonuses highlighted in the text such as *"CR 5 Bonus if characters capture an opponent for questioning."*

Introduction to New England

A land of bitterly cold winters and picturesque autumns bursting with color, New England scenery is often what comes to mind when people think of the good old days of America (something that the tourist industry went to great lengths to cultivate). Quaint little towns and historic monuments from the Revolutionary War are found almost everywhere, and a sense of "down-home America" was often manufactured where it didn't actually exist. Many of the very first conflicts of the Revolutionary War were fought in the New England, engendering a great sense of independence and pride in its residents.

Geography

New England's landscape varies dramatically in a relatively small area. There are small mountains to the north, gentle harbors to the south, expansive lakes in the center and to the west and rocky, jagged coasts to the north. It is the coastline and forests that are the most distinctive features, however. The crooked arm of Massachusetts' Cape Cod is famous nation-wide, and the zig-zag coast of Maine immediately calls to mind images of massive lobsters. At the same time, there are few who have not seen an image of New England in autumn, with its vast forests painted in reds, golds and browns.

Climate

Bitterly cold in the winter and sticky hot in the summer, New England has rather dramatic extremes in weather. Summer temperatures waver between 80 and 90 degrees Fahrenheit, though the humidity makes it seem much worse. Similarly, while winter temperatures usually hover near freezing, strong winds create a wind chill that effectively drops it much lower, even below 0 degrees. Rain is common but not oppressive, it is the winter snowstorms that are remarkable. In northern New England especially, severe snow storms can bury everything under several feet of snow in a single night. Such inclement weather would sometimes halt every-

thing, holding towns and cities at a standstill for a few days even before The End. Now, with manpower and equipment at such a premium, heavy snows can trap unfortunate victims for days, or even weeks in particularly bad cases (See DMG for the effects of bad weather).

Character Involvement

Much of this adventure is written as it would unfold without direct or significant character involvement, to allow Judges to properly tailor the situation to their needs. If players have built characters with the status of lower soldiers, they will have little say in broad decisions and their influence will be limited to their immediate surroundings, as dictated by the orders they receive. Characters that are given leadership roles have a much greater impact, as their decisions direct a large number of men. Any success they achieve may lead to a better outcome than the event summarized in this book, just as their failures could turn this into an even greater tragedy, at the Judge's discretion.

Unspeakable Horror and Irrepressible Rebellion

While ***The End*** itself is a post-apocalyptic game concerned with morality and survival, not all its adventures need to follow the same pattern. New England, with its historic homes, ancient graveyards and tracks of relatively undisturbed wilderness, is a perfect setting for horror. Ghost stories are almost universal, but Lovecraftian horror lends itself to the northeastern spirit with remarkable ease. H.P. Lovecraft actually lived in Rhode Island and many of his stories took place nearby. The dense forests of northern New England may hide horrors unheard of, and the dark seas may hide even more frightful terrors. Judges looking for somewhere to set their horror game should find exactly what they are looking for in the rotting colonial homes, towering lighthouses, isolated cabins or rocky coastline of New England. Who knows where some creature better left undisturbed may slumber away the centuries? What horrors did the Rapture unleash upon the world, or what did it awaken?

The region's association with the Revolutionary War also makes it a fitting backdrop for stories of rebellion and the fight for freedom, themes that are displayed in the Boston colonists, the Sons of Liberty. Ambitious Judges may want to run a campaign where Washington, D.C. is able to conquer New England and the remaining survivors must fight to regain their freedom from their oppressors. The themes of rebellion and the fight for freedom may also be played up in the adventure presented in this book. References to the Revolutionary War are easily inserted (the title of this book is one itself) and the Washington force is already pretty clearly an oppressive enemy. Amplifying the feeling that this is a struggle not simply for survival, but for freedom itself should be relatively simple.

Getting to Boston

The Boston Massacre is written with the assumption that the characters have already arrived in the Boston colony. **Chapter One**, while it does serve an introductory purpose, is designed to familiarize the *players*, and not their *characters*, with the city. ***The End*** is not a game of wandering adventurers overcoming random encounters on their way to retrieving the magic item and rescuing the princess. It *is* a game about community, sacrifice and survival. Characters are, to one extent or another, defined by their role in their community, even

if that is one of "outsider."

In this adventure, characters are assumed to be involved with the community within Boston and involved with the Sons of Liberty and their cause. They may be full members, shouldering their duties as part of the colony, or they may be travelers and traders who come through the area regularly, selling their wares and supplies in return for shelter and companionship. Either way, they must have some sort of stake in Boston and its continued survival, or they will have no logical reason not to simply exit stage left when things get hot. Maybe they live in Boston and don't want to find a new home. Maybe they are in love with one of the residents. Maybe they just need a safe place to weather the tough New England winter. Maybe it's all those and more, but whatever the reason, they need a connection to the city. Instead of providing an explanation that will only work for a few people, I have left that up to the ones who will make the choice that will work best for them – the players and their Judge.

This adventure is not built with a particular party composition in mind. Tailoring it to suit each group's strengths and weaknesses is a matter of shifting emphasis around rather than large-scale changes. *The Boston Massacre* incorporates plenty of opportunities for both combat and role playing, alike. Each Judge should use their discretion with regards to what elements and scenes to give more weight to over others. Keep in mind the capabilities of the characters and the desires of the players and almost any sort of party should fit comfortably into this campaign. **Act I** serves another role in this regard, giving the Judge ample opportunity to gauge what those characters are capable of and plan accordingly.

That said, there are a number of ways to get characters to Boston if necessary. Within New England, virtually all major highways and roads either lead to Boston or come pretty close. Enough road signs remain standing that wandering travelers should not find it too hard to make their way to the city. With a reliable map and some luck, it should be just as easy to travel across the country to New England. If the characters are remarkable enough to have access to more advanced technology (and want to risk their routes remaining open) they can try the train lines that run from various cities around the nation through the New York City area and on to Boston, and there is also both Boston Harbor and the city's Logan Airport. Trying to travel by train or plane in this new world is an adventure in itself, however.

CHAPTER TWO

The Boston Metropolitan Area

History

The history of Boston as an organized colony begins very soon after the Revelation. Within mere weeks the former city had several hundred residents again. It was, after all, the most logical place for Meek from all over New England to travel to, whether in desperate search for supplies or simple companionship. People flocked to the city, but frighteningly few of them really knew how to survive in this new and abandoned world. Certainly none of them were fully prepared for the facts and hardships of this life, not even the charismatic officer Lieutenant Colonel Henry Thomas Jefferson. He did, however, have an idea, one which he readily shared with his fellow citizens of a post-Revelations Boston. He got organized.

Years of military service had provided Jefferson with the skills necessary to survive, the discipline needed to maintain those skills and the powerful charisma required to teach them to others. Freely offering to help other survivors learn how to survive, he began to build a community around himself, carrying on the tradition of something that Jefferson held most sacred in his heart: America. Under his capable leadership, the fledgling colony survived, even thrived. Supplies were scavenged and stockpiled, homes were rebuilt and it looked like electricity could be restored quickly. All of this changed when three strange men came calling on the Lt. Col.

Jefferson's deadly meeting early one morning with the "Three Killers," as the colonists soon began calling them, has taken on a near-legendary status in Boston. He met the three heavily armed men alone and after barely five minutes he walked out, over their corpses. Jefferson said simply that the men were the vanguard of a much larger invading force, but speculation about what "really" happened was rampant, and wild stories of his heroism and martial skill still circulate through Boston. Some say that the men attempted to bribe or threaten Jefferson into giving up the colony without a fight, and he shot them in righteous disgust. According to one story, an old enemy sent the men as a warning of the invasion to come, a "declaration of war" as it was. Washington, D.C., and perhaps even the rest of the East Coast, are under the control of this evil figure, bent on revenge because of some past defeat at Jefferson's hands. Others whisper that the men were the agents of the Devil, and Jefferson beat them down with his honor and his faith, but they only say that very quietly.

Regardless of the events of that night, Lt. Col. Jefferson emerged convinced that a new war was coming to his colony, and it must be prepared. Offering to provide supplies and support for anyone who decided to leave instead of staying to fight, he reputedly nearly burst into tears when none of the survivors took him up on the offer. Like the army they would have to become, the residents of Boston assembled under Jefferson's leadership. No longer were they simply survivors left behind after God's judgment, now they had become the Sons of Liberty, defending the dream and

THE END

tradition of the United States of America even after the end of the world.

The training regimen was strenuous and grueling, but Jefferson knew it had to be if they were going to be prepared in time. It was during this time that Boston began to take on the shape it wears today, that of a recognized government. The success of the colony was not due solely to Jefferson's efforts, however. Beside him from nearly the beginning were Philip Meer and Joseph Meehan; both of whom proved to be invaluable advisors within the political arena. Jefferson had a masterful grasp of tactics and military organization, but if his dream of a new America were to survive into the future, let alone the conflict looming over it, Boston would have to be more than a ragged army fighting for its survival. It had to become a community.

The city's population continued to grow through this period, as more survivors made their way to Boston in a slow but steady trickle. Susan Cominsky joined the colony during this period, and spent much of her time looking for other survivors throughout New England. As the army approached from the south, the trickle increased dramatically with fearful people fleeing northward to a hope for safety and shelter. At its peak, more than eleven hundred lost souls called Boston home, and were preparing to defend it with their lives, if necessary.

During the three weeks before its enemy arrived, a loose collection of desperate survivors evolved into a dedicated, if not experienced, fighting force. Under Jefferson's command, they were as prepared as they could have been when the day finally came. The Battle of Boston was the colony's first, and most decisive, victory, but it was not enough to deter the enemy.

When the armored column of the enemy first rolled into Boston, it had expected resistance. What it found instead was an empty city, seemingly unplundered by its former residents. The looting started almost immediately as the undisciplined but well equipped invading force broke and fell upon the enticing riches the residents of the city had scattered in their path. In the ensuing confusion the Sons of Liberty descended upon their foes, slaughtering several hundred enemy soldiers and suffer almost no losses themselves. Boston rejoiced at their victory, but the greatest benefit was in recovering a great deal of deadly weaponry and vehicles from the defeated force.

Since that initial success, Boston has utilized similar guerrilla tactics, almost always fighting forces with both superior equipment and numbers. A combination of better tactics and discipline has often allowed Boston to carry the day, but sometimes at great price. The colony technically won the tragic Battle of Three Hills far to the south of Boston not long after their initial vic-

Boston at a Glance

Population: 991 (approximately 495 able combatants)
Leader: Lt. Col. Henry Jefferson
Government: Republic
Attitude: Friendly
Electricity: Nominal
Supplies needed: Virtually everything, weapons, medical supplies and manpower

tory, but only after loosing forty-seven citizens and being completely unable to retain control of that territory as enemy reinforcements soon pushed them back. Boston has managed to win nearly all of the battles it fights, but each one claims more and more of its limited citizenry, and the enemy seems to have no end to its army. The colony simply cannot win a battle of attrition— yet it is faced with little alternative. Thus, the Sons of Liberty continue to defend their domain with a resolute desperation.

Geography

Boston's influence on the surrounding area has been severely limited due to the continuing conflict. Fighting a slow retreat, the colony loses a bit of ground with each battle. As a result, the Sons of Liberty are only able to maintain a strong presence within the city of Boston itself. The bordering cities and the suburbs surrounding the metropolitan area are constantly in flux. One will be captured by the invaders one night, only to fall to Boston the next week. None can really be counted as fully under the control of either force, though Washington's army finds it easier to retain the territory they do manage to capture, if only through sheer weight of numbers.

The City of Boston

The center of Boston's power, both symbolically and practically, lies in the heart of the old city, abutting the deteriorating skyscrapers that once dominated the city's skyline. Lt. Col. Jefferson, in a conscious attempt to provide some sense of continuity between the new colony and the old state of Massachusetts, holds virtually all important meetings and councils within the State House. It is a point of pride among the Sons of Liberty that the invaders have never penetrated far enough into the city to launch an attack on this last refuge. Of all of

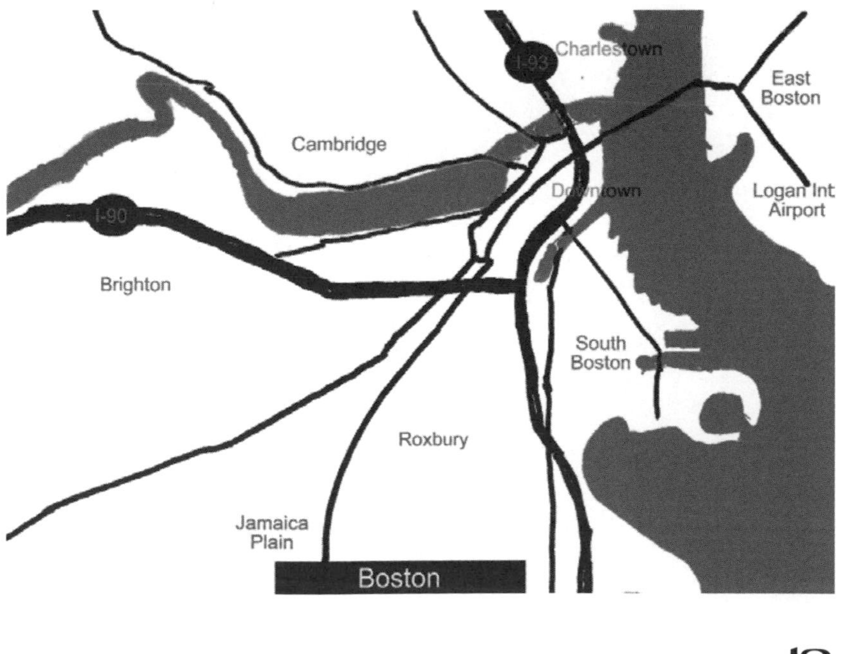

Boston's few permanent facilities, the State House is certainly the busiest, with colonists coming and going constantly during the day and even through the night. Kept meticulously clean and sheltering the colony's government and leaders as it does, the State House has become a solid, tangible symbol of all that it is fighting for— freedom, democracy and its very survival.

Across the street from the political center of Boston is its cultural center, the Boston Common. A sizable park before the end, it has only become more lush and vibrant. The colonists of Boston gather here during their brief periods of calm. Despite an overall ban on music for military reasons, Jefferson has been known to allow an afternoon of revelry when stress is unusually high. The colonists spend the majority of their precious off-duty time enjoying the tranquility of the Commons.

The limited intellectual and religions circles within Boston are centered several blocks west in Copley Square. One of the priests of the impressive Trinity Church survived God's Revelation and found himself among the Meek after the end of the world. Father Trevor Bastin did not lose his faith, however, and he remains in his church, cleaning and offering it to the few residents of the colony who come to pray. He has also taken on the responsibility of maintaining the former Boston Public Library across the square from the Trinity Church, a service that many more people take advantage of. Everyone knows Father Trevor, and he goes to great lengths to help them

find what they need, whether in the library or the church across the square. Whether through a desire to keep the past alive or simply a need to find a quiet method of recreation, almost every member of the colony visits the library on a regular basis. Indeed, Ann and Brendan Burke (a brother and sister who had been studying engineering at MIT when The End came) spend almost every minute they have which is not dedicated to construction in the library. Jefferson's aides are often sent to the library to research military history and tactics in the hope of gaining the upper hand against the colony's enemies.

A little further west lies the colony's highest point and the limit of invader's farthest penetration into Boston during the first battle for the city. The Prudential Center, commonly called "the Prue", looms over above the city around it, an isolated giant, far from the other skyscrapers. This unique vantage point provides a clear view of the city for miles around, a fact that the Sons of Liberty use to their advantage. While scouts posted there certainly cannot see everything, they are in a perfect position to coordinate between the various scouting parties throughout the city. Furthermore, the Prue, prominent and visible from the entire city, has become almost as important a symbol of the colony's survival as the State House. An entire contingent of SOL soldiers is dedicated to the upkeep and occupation of "the Prue."

The citizens of Boston make their homes in the hotels and apartments throughout the city, though they tend to move frequently. During the summer, when the city is warm and sunny, the colonists are very spread out, some even moving their temporary homes all the way out to beyond Kenmore Square and the Boston University dormitories. Surviving families and groups of friends often

find a building to their liking and claim it as their domain, returning there as the seasons change again. In the often bitterly cold winter months, however, the colonists almost crowd together in downtown hotels like the Park Plaza near the State House or the Sheraton in Copley Square. There is more than enough real estate to go around and disputes are extremely rare. When they do occur, Jefferson or the Senate steps in to arbitrate.

The Metropolitan Area

Across the rest of the city, colonists have established supply depots and caches for use in emergencies. Ammunition and basic medical supplies are stashed in cars, buildings, mailboxes and even trash cans sometimes. In a few instances, a building is converted into a larger and more elaborate storehouse to coordinate scavenging and supply efforts for the area around it. The police station in Brighton serves as a center of operations for the areas west of the city, providing supplies for scouts and coordinating the effort to protect Boston's western front. The farther from Boston one gets, the more the buildings become homes and houses as opposed to stores and apartment complexes. The larger roads, particularly are major intersections, have clusters of shops and husks of abandoned businesses, but the rest of the area is a sea of small homes, many with tiny lawns surrounded by fences. Even they begin to thin out and give way to the rapidly encroaching wilderness before long. The quaint homes and inexorable advance of nature makes for something of a peaceful, if rather melancholy, atmosphere in the area.

Along the south in communities like Dorcester and Mattapan, there are no large, central facilities as the constant pressure from the invasion forces makes them impractical. Supplies are instead divided into a larger number of small, well-hidden caches, minimizing the damage should one or more were to be uncovered. The constant fighting in the area has left its mark, many buildings and cars are simply burnt-out husks. Fires ravaged entire blocks after particularly heavy conflicts, leaving some neighborhoods looking like desolate war zones. Residential and business districts alike have been destroyed during the near-constant guerrilla war between the Sons of Liberty and the southern invasion force. Although the cities themselves are not unlike the much more peaceful regions to the northwest, the conflict amid ruins generates an tense air of paranoia and desperation.

The Surrounding Area

The central city of Boston and its metropolitan area are surrounded on all sides by suburbs, many of which are rapidly becoming part of the wilderness, falling to the Blues or being buried under the unnaturally growing forests. Medford and Waltham, not far to the north, are both overrun with thick vegetation and wild animals that no longer hold any fear for man. Rumors abound of great beasts and monsters stalking the forests north of the city and into New Hampshire. To the west the ruins of city of Worcester remains as a crumbling testament to mankind's past. Close enough to be easily reached but distant enough to not have been thoroughly plundered, Worcester is the destination of a number of scavenging expeditions, on both sides of the conflict. More than ones a supply mission has been hijacked. The Sons of Liberty use their knowledge of the area to best advantage and almost always emerge victorious in such skirmishes, especially when the enemy cannot press its numerical advantage.

The Enemy Camp

The army from Washington has set up its camp not even ten miles to the south of Boston, in the city of Quincy. Close enough to the front lines for quick deployment, the encampment also provides security, as it is out of the range of quick raids by the Sons of Liberty. Milton, a bit further north, is also a primary center of power for the army. It was quickly captured and secured early in the campaign. Now it functions as an essential staging ground for further assaults on Boston territory.

Originally following Route 95 along the coast from New York to Boston, the Washington army still makes extensive use of the highway. Not only does it skirt around the city, a feature the invaders use to flank around the Sons of Liberty to strike at the western front, but it also leads directly into the major city of Providence, to the south. The army is composed almost entirely of combatants, and thus relies heavily upon scavenging to provide supplies, stores and food. During the ongoing war with Boston, the Washington force has returned to Rhode Island again and again to plunder it to fulfill its needs. The army has, in fact, paid little attention to the surrounding land, such as the cities of Connecticut or even the closer Cape Cod. Instead it has focused entirely upon dealing with the Boston colony first and foremost, leaning upon the ruins of Providence to maintain itself while doing so.

Other Places of Note

Not everything in the area is under the dominion of the Sons of Liberty or the force opposing them, however. The colonists in Boston are fighting a desperate battle for survival and are barely able to hold on to their present territory, let alone expand it. At the same time, the army from Washington has concentrated its attention on destroying the colony, as well as foraging expeditions into the ruined cities to the south, such as Providence. This leaves a fair amount of land open for the taking while the two giants in the area struggle against each other.

Encounter Tables for Wilderness Areas

Judges should check for encounters every 2 hours on the following table:

D20	Result
1	Recently Deceased Human (Plague Victim, if examined make check for infection by Lyon's Plague, The End, p. 209).
2	Rag Tag Patrol (2-4 standard scouts from the Biker Army, See Appendix C).
3	Snake-Poisonous (See MM).
4	Bear (See MM).
5	Wolf Pack (2-4 Wolves, See MM).
6	Wanderers (2-5 Refugees, either from New York or elsewhere, See Appendix C).
7-20	No Encounter.

The Judge should adjust this basic table to reflect to relative remoteness of any given area or its proximity to certain groups. For example, if the characters are near the The Enemy Camp, the animal encounters may be replaced with Rag tag encounters.

Once the conflict is resolved, however, the victor will turn to address any other settlements – a concern that has led some otherwise neutral parties to sell their services to both sides, trying to keep the conflict going for as long as possible.

To the east of the center of Boston, across a section of the harbor, lies the old city's Logan airport. A massive, sprawling complex, Logan was constantly bustling with activity before The End, with flights coming and going at all times of the day and night. Now the facility stands empty, dark and ominously quiet. Despite the vast space and easily defensible location it presents, no one has ever settled there, at least anyone who was ever heard from again. One small contingent of hopeful settlers, about a dozen strong men and women, moved to claim the airport as their domain soon after the Revelation, shortly before Jefferson established the Boston colony to defend the area against Washington. They were never heard from again after the first night, nor were any bodies discovered when concerned Boston residents went to look for them. When a number of searchers also disappeared in the night, the Bostonians got the message and left the entire peninsula alone. Residents of the area tell fanciful stories about the lost "Logan Colony" and the vengeful ghosts that haunt it, but no one dares to be caught there after dark. Something is there, and it doesn't want company.

Other dangers are more readily evident. The Lechmere mall, at the end of the Green Line of the subway system that runs throughout the city and the surrounding area, is the home to what most colonists consider a dangerous and insane cult. As they are occupied with the Washington army and the cultists are across the Charles River in Cambridge, however, Boston has made no move against the encampment. A bloody congregation of less than ten survivors led by a darkly charismatic leader who insists on being called "the Prophet," members of the Lechmere cult pray to Satan as a savior, to rescue them now that God has turned his back. Concentrating on performing small animal sacrifices or reveling one form of debauchery or another, the cult supports itself entirely on scavenging and raiding. It has given both Boston and the invaders a wide berth, however, fully aware that either could easily crush it.

Not far from the cult's domain lies the campus of Harvard University. In the early period of the conflict, the university buildings were used as supply depots for northern expeditions. Within the last month, however, a number of caches have apparently been uncovered and looted, causing Jefferson to order northern supplies stored in the west, in the Brighton depots. Scouts have also reported noticing an increasing number of strangers in the area around Harvard, and nearly everyone catches a glimpse of movement or feels like they are being watched when in the vicinity. Susan Cominsky and many of her scouts are convinced that a new and secret colony, likely a very tiny one, has settled in the area, but Jefferson remains unconvinced. He thinks that it is highly unlikely that any significant group of people could move into the area without being noticed and identified. The truth, however, remains unclear and is likely to remain so, as Boston has no resources to dedicate to uncovering it.

Resources

The ruins of a vast metropolis like Boston are a rich prize to plunder, undoubtedly one of the reasons that Washington is so eager to occupy it.

The city is not necessarily an easy place to live in, however, and its stores are not unlimited. The invasion force has relied heavily upon scavenging to support itself, leaving many of the cities to the south depleted, at least in part. The colony itself has been forced to divert attention from subsistence to defense ever since Jefferson's fateful encounter with the Three Killers, also growing to rely on scavenging more and more as the conflict stretches on.

Although recovering preserved foodstuffs throughout the area provides a significant portion of Boston's food, it is not the only avenue open to the colony. The city has always been a port town with an extensive harbor, a fact unchanged by the End, even if nature has become even more unpredictable. One of the survivors living in Boston when Jefferson founded his colony was an experienced fisherman, and he has trained a handful of people in the trade to the extent that the colony is actually able to field a tiny fishing fleet of three vessels. While they do not return with massive quantities of fish and are unable to make use of many modern methods, seafood does have a central place in the Bostonian diet. Further afield and with a bit more difficulty, the colony makes regular use of the encroaching wilderness to the north in New Hampshire for hunting expeditions. Dear, rabbit and a variety of wild game are a welcome treat by the weary Sons of Liberty. However, predators have become more common and more vicious. The conflict with Washington has diverted much of the colony's attention away from gathering or growing food, placing salvaged canned or non-perishable food high on the list of foraging parties. Finding food in Boston itself requires a Scavenge check (DC 17), though it may vary at the Judge's discretion. Scavenging in the surrounding countryside or neighboring cities may be much easier or much more difficult, depending on how thoroughly they have been looted, or whether they

have fallen prey to the Blues.

Weaponry has never been plentiful in the area, however. The colonists have raided and scavenged from gun stores and police departments, coming away with small arms and ammunition, but they are completely outgunned by the invasion force. Worse, the closest military base to downtown Boston was apparently decommissioned right before the Fourth Seal was broken. The training and discipline of the SOL soldiers does go a long way to make up this discrepancy, and when victorious, the Sons have managed to strengthen their armory with higher-grade equipment taken from their foes. For the most part they must make do with that they have. Soldiers in heavy fighting on the southern front are given the best weapons, sometimes even military rifles, while other citizens have handguns or hunting rifles at most. A reliable supply of advanced weaponry would dramatically help the SOL cause (but not nearly so much as a reliable supply of people). Those searching for weapons in locations likely to have a supply (jails, police stations, gun stores) face a DC 20 Scavenge check, due to how thoroughly they have already been searched. Condition will be Worn at best.

The colony is desperate for more warm bodies to carry on the fight against the invasion force. Boston is winning most of the battles, but losing the war. The enemy can afford to send wave after wave of soldiers and does not seem to care about sacrificing so many people. Washington is fighting a long war of attrition, and it can apparently afford to. Boston cannot. Unfortunately for the Sons of Liberty, few people want to throw their lot into an area at war. The rapid growth that marked the days before Washington's first attack are long gone and Jefferson is watching his proud colony get slowly ground down. Defense of the city is foremost on the Lt. Col.'s mind, and it is becoming increasingly clear that he may not be able to win this war without reinforcements. To that end, Jefferson is almost desperate to establish a lasting political and military alliance with another colony to defeat the invaders. He is worried that will be the only viable option.

Due to the conflict with Washington, Boston has had little time to devote to repairing the city's infrastructure. They have no electricity or running water or any such amenities. The Burke siblings worked to repair one of the city's power generators for a while and had almost succeeded when the attacks started. Now they have been forced to concentrate on repairing equipment and securing fuel and supplies. Most of the colony's gasoline has come from abandoned gas stations that have yet to be destroyed or completely looted. They have yet to find any sort of regional depot or large storage station. Such a find would be a godsend, however, allowing the colonists to dramatically increase their maneuverability and speed with an entire fleet of vehicles.

Residents

The Meek living in Boston are a hardy and often grim lot. Life in the colony is not easy, the war is omnipresent with a new skirmish or conflict every few days. Living after the Revelation is hard enough, and these battles only make it worse. The Sons of Liberty don't have electricity beyond gas powered generators to heat or light their homes and most often cannot afford to make fires for fear of attracting the attention of the invaders. Winters in New England are harsh and unforgiving; the snow is high and the temperatures low.

The colonists stubbornly persist,

however. Boston is their home, and they are determined to see it kept free, free from the tyranny of Washington, D.C. Lt. Col. Jefferson himself was an intensely patriotic man, serving the nation he loved in defense of the ideal of liberty, and the colony he founded sees itself as the inheritor of that tradition. "God may have abandoned us, but we have not abandoned the self-evident truths of liberty, equality and justice," Jefferson has told his followers, and they took it to heart. The image of upholding the tradition of a proud nation in this dangerous world is very important to Boston, forming the center of their morale. American flags are treasured and the state house is used to house the colony's small government.

Government

Lt. Col. Jefferson could have easily declared himself king of Boston, especially after the fighting began and he led his people to victory after victory. However, Jefferson has gone to great lengths to ensure that he is not considered a king. The first thing he did after providing every colonist with basic combat training was to establish a government in keeping with his democratic ideals. He called for the colony to establish a formal governing body for itself and elect representatives to it. After a great deal of discussion, a tiny senate was formed and seven representatives were elected to it via secret ballot. Jefferson was, of course, unanimously voted into the group and has effectively taken on the role of chairman and generally recognized leader of the colony, even though a man by the name of David Tarr actually holds the title of president. What worries Jefferson most is that few people ever challenge his authority. Jefferson has been very vocal about how he views this senate as a temporary measure, an interim government while Boston remains under siege. When the invaders are defeated, he assures the colony, a real government can be established. Few of the Sons seem concerned.

Jefferson, Philip Meer and Joseph Meehan are by far the most influential members of the council. All of the senators are still only in the beginning of their first terms in office.

Religion

Faith in Boston is a quiet thing. Religion has an odd place all across the world after the End, and the colonists in Boston hardly have the luxury of time to dedicate to untangling the theological problems of the world after God's departure. Only Father Bastin and a few others openly proclaim faith in the Lord. Others are very resentful of both God and his believers. Friction between those who blame their current troubles on God and Father Bastin's followers is the primary cause of unrest within the colony. This has never progressed to open violence, but it has created a great deal of bad blood in the small population. Otherwise peaceful meals and gatherings have been shattered, devolving into shouting matches between devout believers on either side. Most of those living in Boston still find themselves praying to God in the heat of battle, even if they cannot understand why He has abandoned them and the world.

Given Boston's current situation, locked in combat with a superior foe, the colonists have little time for alternative religions. There may be shamans or magicians living among the smaller, more mysterious settlements in the area, such as in the Lechmere Mall or Logan Airport, but they have not attracted any significant attention. Boston has much more immediate and pressing issues to attend to.

Who's Who

Full d20 game information can be found on each of the following in Appendix C. Judges should embellish or reduce character's history or roles as they see fit.

Lt. Col. Henry Thomas Jefferson (Meek/Thug/Founder)

Born into a family with a proud tradition of patriotic support of the land of the free and the home of the brave, you took on the mantle your father and your father's father had worn, serving with distinction in the military. After graduating with honors from West Point in 1970, you fought in every war America was involved in, larger or small. From the horrors of Vietnam to peacekeeping operations in trouble spots scattered across the globe, you were always on the front lines, leading the fight to defend your beloved nation and the ideals it held dear. America came before everything else, including God.

Even after the End, your passionate dedication to democracy and the values set down in the Constitution did not waver at all. Your training left you better suited to survive in this new world than most, and you soon began to train anyone who would learn. At first you were simply struggling to survive and doing your best to help others do the same, but then you began to dream of something more as you saw a settlement form and America was reborn before your eyes. Then you met with three men who wanted to "parley."

Now you find yourself at the helm of a desperate colony facing what is apparently a much larger and better-equipped force. Watching your fellow colonists fight for their freedom has only fanned the flames of your passion - you can see a new America being born in Boston. The war deeply worries you, however, not only for the conflict itself but also for what will happen afterward. Already you chafe under the responsibility and adoration you receive. Politics have always made you uncomfortable and you have done everything in your power to avoid being put in any position as king of Boston, even if it's called the "presidency."

Role playing notes: An powerful and imposing man, you are level-headed and even somewhat reserved, except when defending the ideals of liberty you hold so dear. Then it is nearly impossible to conceal the passion and emotion within you. You are worried about your position in the colony, concerned that other residents place too much onto you and not the dream you follow. Exercise your near-total influence over Boston with caution and only in the rarest of circumstances.

Appearance: Despite being nearly fifty, Jefferson cuts an impressive figure. Always carrying a very dignified air, his attire is perpetually neat and clean. He is the very image of the righteous general, well-kept hair framing a deeply lined face and piercing eyes.

Traits: strong, tough, charismatic, highly skilled.

Philip Meer (Meek/Founder)

You were always concerned with the little things, perhaps to the exclusion of the "big picture." After a cautious and calculated college program in history, you led a cautious and calculated career at Harvard University and had two cautious and calculated marriages. One divorce couldn't force you to see the forest for the tress, what hope did a second have?

It took the end of the world to jar you loose, and by then everyone you loved was gone. If it hadn't been for Lt. Col. Jefferson and his dream of a free colony to fight for, you might not have survived in a world abandoned by God. From the beginning, Jefferson's burning passion and charisma gave you something to fight and work for, until his vision became your own. You have been by his side from the beginning, taking care of the details of founding and running a colony, following Jefferson devotedly and without question. As the second most prominent and respected member of the Boston senate, however, the Lt. Col.'s apparent fear of truly taking on the leadership role for the colony has begun to greatly concern you. Someone is going to have to lead Boston and take on the responsibility

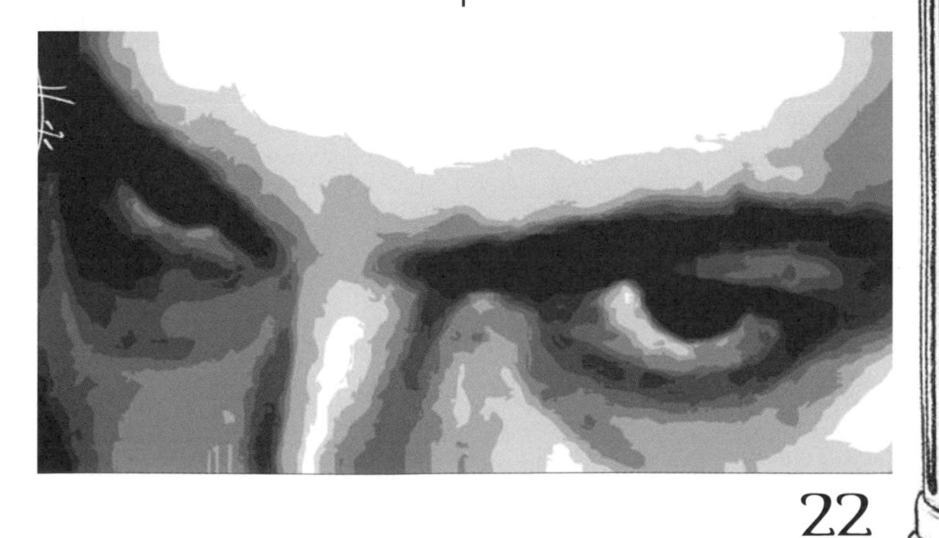

such a position would entail, and you have just begun to flex your political influence. Jefferson is a great man, but you have begun to doubt if he is the right man.

Role playing notes: You are still concerned with details, but they do not rule you. Ironically enough, it took The End of the world to allow you to enjoy life. You are cautious and thoughtful, but not a coward by any stretch of the imagination. When action is called for, you can and will leap into the midst of it all just as fast as anyone else.

Appearance: Middle-aged and balding, Meer was a history professor and looked the part, but surviving in the End has worn the stereotype away. An embarrassing gut has been replaced with wiry muscle, giving the small man to body of someone a decade his junior.

Traits: Wise, intelligent

Joseph Meehan (Meek)

You knew it was going to happen, the terrible visions of apocalypse that wracked your dreams slowly crept into the corner of even your waking hours until the End finally came and the world was damned. Of course, you tried to tell them, but they wouldn't listen to you. Nothing you could do would convince them or prevent what was coming. The Baltimore newspaper you worked for sent you on "vacation" and recommended that you visit a psychiatrist. Your parents would only look at you with their eyes full of pity and your girlfriend simply left you. Eventually, you even doubted yourself. Being proven right was really no consolation at all.

Surviving in this new world was a difficult task, and when a new empire quickly rose in Washington, D.C. and spread to the surrounding area, it was obvious resistance was futile, so you didn't bother. When your commander told you to go north and infiltrate Boston, you knew refusing would mean your death, so you didn't bother to argue. Arriving in Boston, however, you found peace for the first time since the visions of the End struck you. Jefferson's energy and the hope of the entire colony were contagious and you began to feel at home, becoming a center of the new city. Then the invasion force destroyed those dreams and you realized how foolish it was to have thought of freedom in the first place. With the invaders came a new vision of another apocalypse, one in which a massive pentagon and a horrific man covered in blood loom on a dark horizon, eclipsing everything. The message is obvious: it is impossible to stop the coming horror, so why bother trying?

Role playing notes: Despite your position in Boston's senate, you know that this war cannot be won and struggling against Washington just means more death on all sides. You fight like all of your fellows, at least for now, but only because you have been ordered to. Very soon you will be forced to betray your new home, and you know it. If only there was some way to stop fate and fight against destiny…

Appearance: Until the visions began anew just recently, Meehan was a striking young man with striking features. Tall, dark and handsome, he was even more charismatic and moving than Jefferson, providing a youthful and vigorous counterpart to the Lt. Col.'s passion and Meer's caution on the council. He has become more and more withdrawn and melancholy of late, however, something that most who know him attribute to the stress of the conflict with the invaders.

Traits: charismatic, perceptive.

David Tarr (Meek)

You went to business school because your parents wanted you to. You joined the firm because your wife wanted you to. You joined the PTA and became its president because your kids wanted you to. You can't remember the last time you did something because *you* wanted to – and then it was too late because the world ended. You were amazed that life went on, however. Even after The End, you still got hungry and cold and tired. You were completely unprepared for this new and terrible world and would have died if one of Lt. Col Jefferson's students hadn't found you and brought you to the fledgling colony. Jefferson's training saved your life and gave you a chance to do something for yourself, and you'll never forget that.

When Jefferson asked you to become the President of this colony, you were stunned. Politics had always been your dream, but your parents felt it was too unstable and your wife had hated the idea of living so public a life. You leapt at the chance, excited to finally be able to do something because *you* wanted to for a change. It soon became clear who truly lead the colony, however. Despite the title, Jefferson is still in charge and virtually unchallenged. You have begun to worry if you are just a figurehead, and if becoming President was really what you wanted, or if it was what Jefferson wanted.

Role playing notes: Quiet, withdrawn and increasingly pensive, you no longer feel so certain and assured of your actions. Increasingly you wonder if you really want to be a President who does nothing, and you wonder if Jefferson put you there intentionally. You have become suspicious that he is hiding something, and that is why he avoids officially taking control of the colony.

Appearance: Before The End, he was the cookie-cutter image of millions of other white-faced businessmen. His hair is still receding and thinning and he still wears small, professional glasses, but the realities of life after the Rapture has slimmed him down considerably and given him a much more weathered look.

Traits: Quiet, highly observant, suspicious.

Jaime Dahlke (Meek/Physician)

The only son of a hard-working industrial worker, you clawed your way up from poverty to work your way through medical school, determined to make a difference. Somewhere along the way, you got lost. School was just too expensive, and your dreams of becoming a world-famous surgeon or discovering a cure for cancer crumbled. When The End came, you were caring for invalids and the elderly in a facility on Cape Cod.

Ironically, The End was the best thing that could have happened to you. Suddenly you were able to truly do what you had always wanted – to really make a difference. Doctors are valued above almost all other people in this forsaken world, and now you can truly help the people. Boston welcomed you with open arms, thankful to have anyone with advanced medical training. The only problem was Jefferson's impassioned devotion to democracy and the "American Dream." After living in poverty for much of your life and working yourself to the bone to achieve your dream, only to have it snatched from you for something as unimportant as money, you have no faith in a democracy "for the people" that fails to help the people. Communism is the only way to protect everyone's rights and allow for equality. Russia fell to the corruption that was simply accepted as standard operating procedure in the old America. Perhaps this new world, this new Eden, will provide a chance to establish a pure communist state.

Role playing notes: You are friendly and warm, genuinely caring for everyone, even total strangers. That is, after, all why you studied medicine in the first place – to help people. The only thing that you are somewhat guarded and reserved about is politics. Jefferson is obviously an idealist blind to the truth of his dream, but he is also the only hope Boston has for survival, so you keep silent for now.

Appearance: Dahlke is almost always laughing or smiling. He gives a strong and warm handshake with surprisingly thick hands for a doctor, and his small pipe is rarely far. Caring for Boston's sick and wounded leaves him little time to care for his appearance, but he usually has reasonably clean clothes, though they are often creased from the short naps he takes whenever he has the chance to relax.

Traits: intelligent, dexterous, medical skills, political skills

Susan Cominsky (Meek)

Living a life of privilege was easy, you never had to do anything you didn't want to. College and a career in some or other field was just something to do to keep from being bored. That was what everything was, actually. The country always held a special lure for you, though. Whether racing a horse through the woods or just relaxing in the weekend house in Maine, the country was one of the few things you really loved. It was your one true passion in a life of luxury. Then you watched entire family die before your eyes while the whole world went to Hell.

The easy life is gone now, and the natural world is no longer the same. Where once it was beautiful and peaceful, now it is wild and dangerous. You love it just the same, however, and spend more time alone in the area around Boston than in the colony itself, something that you know scares many of your fellow colonists. You do your best to help your fellow survivors, however, and even find their reactions amusing. Relaxing in the city, whether sleeping with someone for a night or speaking about the future in the Commons, is almost as invigorating as traveling through the encroaching forests. Susan Cominsky has found her new life after the end of the world to be much more fulfilling, despite the hardship. The End burned away the dilettante when her family died, leaving behind a woman with the will to survive.

Role playing notes: Life is about enjoying yourself, and even the end of the world can't change that, though now you know that it is not something to simply taken but instead must be worked for. Laughter, joy and beauty are built from blood, sweat and tears. Watching your father, mother and siblings die one by one as The End approached has left its mark on you, however. Your forays into the wilderness is as much driven by a fear of

watching those you care for suffer again as by your love of nature.

Appearance: Cominsky was always beautiful, even as a young girl. Survival after the End has given her lines and hardened her beauty, but not diminished it. Muscular and willful, she still possesses the cultured mind of a socialite, speaking with an unexpected eloquence.

Traits: Strong, great endurance, nimble.

Rebecca Richards (Meek/Founder)

You still remember you husband and your children, and your children's children. You can still remember how much you loved it when they all came over to visit your house in New York City. Nothing gave you as much pleasure as taking care of your family, and you were always the perfect housewife and grandmother. The memories are as fresh as if they happened just yesterday, despite the fact that all of your beloved children and grandchildren have gone on to a better place now (you hope).

In the remains of New York, you became a grandmother to all of the survivors, caring for everyone you could find. When the men with guns came from the south and demanded that everyone throughout the city surrender, you began to worry. When they brutally crushed the little opposition they encountered, you were terrified. You gathered as many people as you could and fled to Boston. You had heard a few stories about it, and it was a large city, sure to have a colony of its own far from these violent invaders. Too bad you were wrong.

Role playing notes: You will *not* see anyone under your care suffer, it is just not acceptable. The fear that not all of your children were virtuous enough to ascend to Heaven and sit with God terrifies you, and you blame yourself for not raising them better. That mistake will not happen again, and you will go to any length to protect the people you have adopted as your new family, even if it means you will die.

Appearance: An elderly woman with thinning, gray hair pulled back into tight bun, Richards almost looks more like a lawyer than a grandmother. She is stern and harsh when worried about her charges, but quickly becomes warm and friendly when able to relax.

Traits: intelligent, wise.

Thaddeus O'Malley (Meek/Thug)

Coming to America to escape the terror and hatred in Ireland, you quickly built your own little piece of the American Dream in New York. Owning and managing *The Emerald Briar* was that dream come true. You thought of yourself as a good Catholic, you saw nothing wrong with being gay and prayed to God to give thanks for all you had. He must not have heard, because when The End came, you were left behind.

You had never given up before, however, and you certainly weren't going to then wither, even when your city was invaded. When Rebecca Richards began to gather other survivors to flee to Boston, you threw yourself into helping her, acting as one of the primary scouts on the journey and providing your own Land Rover to help carry the weaker refugees. You believed Richards' promises of a new life in a new city, away from the troubles of New York. Boston wasn't everything you had hoped for and was mired in a war of its own, but you're not about to quit now, after you've come so far.

Role playing notes: "Never say die." That's the motto you live by and it has served you well enough. Keep your eyes on the prize and don't stop until you simply can't move anymore.

That doesn't leave much time to actually enjoy yourself, however. There is always something that needs to be done, and when you do get a chance to relax, you simply want to enjoy the peace and quiet. The Irish stereotype of the boisterous drunkard amuses you to no end.

Image: Thin, tall and completely bald, O'Malley doesn't look like the typical Irishman either. Before The End, he always kept his clothes immaculate, but now he has to settle for simply cleaner than almost everyone else.

Walton Norfleet (Meek/Thug)

When one of your most promising and charismatic reporters suddenly started ranting about the end of the world and the coming apocalypse, you shook your head and assumed he had gone around the bend. "Take a vacation," you told him. "Get yourself some help." If you have listened to him, you couldn't have stopped The End, but at least you could have prepared yourself and come out of it better. It is, after all, all about coming "out of it" better than everyone else. It was only natural to join the force in Washington, D.C., then. The empire ruled by a bloody man-god would dominate the entire East Coast soon enough, and it is better to be stepping on someone than get stepped upon.

Despite no military training before the apocalypse, the role of soldier suited you well and you rose among the ranks very quickly, always making sure to properly deal with those who helped you up along the way. Before long, in fact, you were given an army and put in charge of "dealing with" the troublesome colony in Boston. Immediately you ordered Joseph Meehan, that very reporter who had heralded the end of the world, to travel to Boston make himself an essential part of the colony. After you had gathered your troops and assisted in the initial operations around New York, you moved on to your target. Jefferson's little colony proved to be much more difficult than you had anticipated, however, and your lack of training in military tactics has become apparent. You are winning this war, but only through a bloody campaign of attrition, and one that does not serve to engender a great deal of loyalty in your troops and officers.

Role playing notes: You are the most important person in your life, that's just common sense, after all. Anything you can do to better your position you will do, and you expect anyone else to do just the same. It's not like you're totally uncaring, but if you don't look out for number one, who will? You are beginning to worry, however, that you are not ready for a military operation of this magnitude. Even more frightening is the question of whether your superiors already knew that when they sent you here.

Image: Stern, dignified and stoic, Norfleet is the perfect images of a reserved and wise general, especially in his sharply cut uniform. His face and attitude betray nothing of his calculating and conniving nature, projecting only a respectable image.

CHAPTER THREE

New England

Massachusetts

Although Boston is the center of Massachusetts and even the entirety of New England, it is not the only location of interest. Forty miles west of the massive metropolis, the remains of Worcester sit in the middle of a web of highways and major roads. Most of the survivors who found themselves in Worcester quickly moved to Boston for the relative safety of the larger colony. In the face of Washington's attacks, however, a small number have returned, hoping to escape to a more peaceful region. Worcester has become more important as a large source of supplies near to the beleaguered and besieged Boston colony. The primary route between Boston and Worcester, I-90, is carefully guarded by the colonists, and fortunately for them the Rag Tag army has concentrated its attention on Boston proper or scavenging in Providence to the south. Were Worcester to be taken from Boston, however, it would be another massive blow to the colony's chance to survive its war.

Further west, the raw wilderness has stretched south from Vermont and New Hampshire, turning western Massachusetts and the Berkshires into a renewed natural wonderland. The region has yet to become as hostile or deadly as the forests of northern New England, and travel through it is actually tranquil and relaxing (a very rare thing after the End).

To the east of Boston is the crooked peninsula of Cape Cod. Living almost entirely on the tourist trade before the Rapture, the Cape was famous for its beaches and whale watching tours. Even after the End, whales are still seen as omens of great fortune among the scattered settlements surviving in the area. At the very tip of the "arm" of the peninsula is the small colony in Provincetown. Almost completely isolated from the rest of New England, except for travel down the entire Cape or by boat across the bay, the 40-odd survivors in the city were forced to band together very quickly in order to survive, and they have managed to establish a thriving, if small and remote, colony.

An ambitious group has made the former tourist trap of Martha's Vineyard into their home. Barely two dozen of the Meek, many of them professional or amateur sailors, have struggled hard to master the new and fickle oceans. They have had some degree of success, so much so that they are able to survive by trading with another small settlement in Hyannis on the southern coast of the Cape and the factions in Newport, Rhode Island. With a handful of small ships, the Vineyard fleet hopes to unite the many disparate groups scattered around America's Atlantic coast, though they are fearful of the increasingly dangerous ocean and its inhabitants. If they are able to reach Boston and come to some sort of alliance, their ability to carry both people and information with remarkable efficiency would be a godsend to the resistance effort.

Connecticut

Connecticut holds little of interest in the new world. Any settlements that would have formed were crushed beneath the inexorable advance of the Washington forces on their way to Boston. Indeed, the entire state has become nothing more than a road from Boston to New York and the rest

of the nation. The central city of Hartford sits at the junction of two major highways and still has a surprising amount of supplies left undisturbed, despite the volume of people who have passed through it. Most travelers recognize its vital importance as a crossroads, a stop on the way to a more distant destination. A number of small shelters and supply depots have been established, fortified and expanded by many of the later visitors who use Hartford. Hartford's central location has turned it into the "Diggers' City" because scavengers and nomads in New England make their way through it on a regular basis, often leaving news or information at one of the supply depots or meeting spots, to be picked up and disseminated by other travelers.

Of further interest in Connecticut are the ruins of Groton, on the coast near the eastern edge of the state. Unremarkable in itself, Groton hosts a US submarine base. The equipment and raw materials inside have weathered the months since The End remarkably well (Good condition) and would be a staggering find for anyone to stumble across it. Weapons, military rations and medical supplies are plentiful, and a particularly adventurous Judge may allow boats or even a submarine to have survived the tribulations and the Blues.

Sleepy Hollow and the Salem Witch Trials

Not more than a half hour drive from Boston lies the Sleepy Hollow Cemetery, in the town of Concord. About the same distance in the other direction is the infamous Salem. Witches on one side and ghosts on the other, Boston is in strange company. With the return of magic and monsters to the world in the wake of God's departure, the tales associated with these two locations are almost too enticing to pass up. Judges looking for an excuse to introduce more supernatural elements into their ***The End*** game need to make little effort if they divert their campaign to these universally recognizable symbols of horror and the paranormal.

Rhode Island

The tiny state of Rhode Island is dominated by the ruined metropolis of Providence. Once a bustling city, it is now relegated to the ignoble role of being the larder for the army from Washington, D.C.. Unable to spare many resources to long range scavenging or even cultivation, the army has returned again to Providence's stores and markets, grabbing everything and anything of value. Despite Providence's size and lack of settlements to further drain its resources, the city has nearly run dry under the strain of supporting an entire army in the midst of a pitched battle to the north. Scavenging for any sort of supplies at all is almost impossible in Providence, and the empty city is crumbling at an amazing rate. Almost empty of anything of any value at all, Providence seems to be in a hurry to decay into dust and blow away on the wind.

Further south, on an island in the irregular Narragansett Bay, lies the city of Newport. Renown for its ostentatious displays of wealth and privilege before The End, the survivors have carried on that tradition in a sick, twisted fashion. Four different factions have laid claim to four of the massive mansions in Newport, and fight a constant and bloody campaign against each other for the limited resources on the island. All bridges off the island have been destroyed, as have most boats. The residents have turned on each other like trapped wolves.

New Hampshire

Largely overrun with rapidly growing forests, New Hampshire does have a number of small settlements, most of them scattered around Lake Winnipesaukee. Few, if any, have more than a dozen members and all of them are too busy surviving to explore the area around them or form significant alliances with other groups. Manchester, what used to be New Hampshire's largest city, lies completely and conspicuously empty and abandoned. There are no settlements or colonies there and only the most experienced diggers and scavengers go in and make it out alive. A number of legends and superstitions have grown up around the deadly city, and the remaining residents of the state blame it on the so-called "America's Stonehenge," a network of tunnels and standing stones long thought to be some sort of ancient sacrificial altar. As of yet, they have made only minor progress, but their limited supernatural might is enough to secure their safety during their travels.

The seaport city of Portsmouth is a very quiet, secretive and tiny colony, intent on unlocking the secrets of the magic that has returned in full force after the Rapture. Thirteen men, all formerly scientists, preachers or doctors before The End, live like monks in the picturesque city, surviving on whatever food they can scavenge while they study any and all texts they are able to locate in both public and private libraries all across nearby cities and towns. Furthermore, they make the trek across half the state to "America's Stonehenge" four times yearly, hoping to find something of supernatural significance there.

Vermont

The verdant forests that cover Vermont's gentle Green Mountains have been almost entirely abandoned to the animals. There are no major settlements across the entire state with the notable exception of Wilson Castle in the small town of Rutland, situated a bit to the south of the center of the state. Ruled over by a madman who insists on being referred to as King Wilson, the settlement of a few hundred people is in something of a precarious situation. The feral wilderness encroaches on all sides and many of the beasts of Vermont have grown particularly vicious since The End, only Wilson Castle and seemingly the King himself can keep them at bay. Each and every individual who has publicly challenge the mad King's authority has later been found dead, coincidentally mauled by beasts. The surviving citizens of Rutland and the area around have been cowed into

Seabrook Nuclear Power Station

Built on the tiny New Hampshire coast despite almost universal protest, the Seabrook Nuclear Power Station never did seem to work quite as intended. Outwardly, the facility appears to have weathered the Rapture well, but no one has yet been brave or foolhardy enough to investigate. By far the region's largest and most controversial nuclear power plant, Seabrook's safety systems should have automatically shut down or sealed off anything dangerous. The world of ***The End*** is not always reliable or logical, however, and almost anything may have happened inside its ominous stacks.

submission, and King Wilson rules over them like a despot, maintaining a life of amazing luxury in this post-apocalypse world.

The rest of Vermont is well and truly under the domain of nature. Man should be wary when traveling through the state, as even the mundane beasts have grown to frightening size and ferocity. The safest routes are usually the shortest, and staying close to the rapidly crumbling roads offers some measure of protection, at least while they last.

Maine

Even more so than Vermont, the former state of Maine is truly a land of new beasts and magic. As large as the rest of the New England states combined, the wilderness is vast and terrible this far north. Where Vermont may harbor dangerous animals, the forests of Maine have an almost unbearable air of menace. It always feels as if something is watching from the darkness amid the trees, something much more *intelligent* than the unnaturally large wolves that might attack travelers through the rest of New England. With the Rapture, frightening things came to Maine, and they have claimed its forests and unbroken wilderness as their home.

Perpetually locked under a thick blanket of snow during the winter, Maine blossoms into growth during the summer months, as if making up for lost time. In this harsh and unforgiving climate, only two settlements of note have managed to survive. To the south, not far from the remains of Maine's biggest city, Portland, the Sabbathday Lake Shaker Community still manages to survive as it has for nearly three centuries. Though they numbered only seven before the End, their numbers have swelled to just shy of one hundred, as they extend their charity to those who are willing to work hard and accept the simple, religious lifestyle of a Shaker. Despite God's apparent abandonment of the

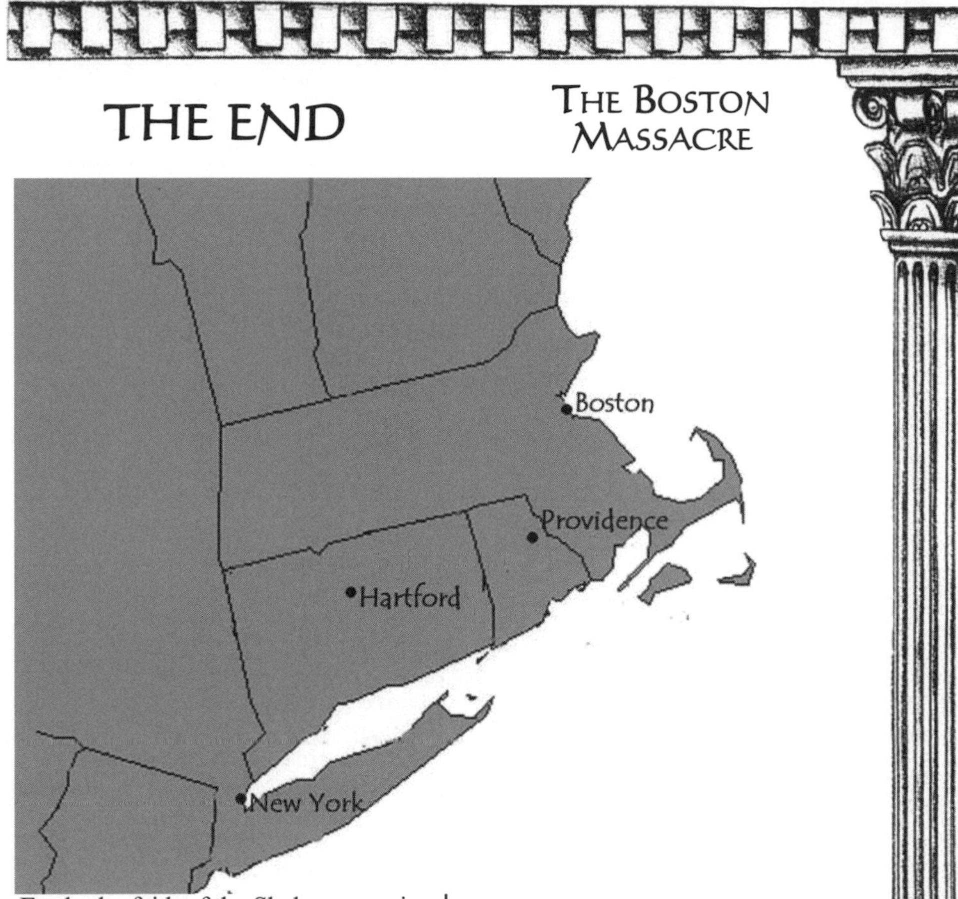

Earth, the faith of the Shakers remains strong, almost palpable in the air of the small, rustic settlement.

About halfway up the coast of Maine, another small settlement has survived, huddled in the massive and impenetrable Fort Knox. Using the fort as a safe and secure base of operations, the tiny colony has gone to great lengths to seek out any survivors in other cities and towns and bring them to safety. Originally formed around a core of survivalists and farmers, it has grown into a hard-bitten encampment. Its 50-odd members have seen and survived almost unspeakable horrors and take no nonsense from anyone. Extremely suspicious of anyone exhibiting even vaguely supernatural abilities, Fort Knox colonists also extend every courtesy and hospitality they can to refugees or visitors. Anyone who can bring news of the state of the world beyond Maine is particularly appreciated.

CHAPTER FOUR: The Boston Massacre

ACT I: THE SET-UP

The Mastiffs of War

As the characters fulfill their portion of patrol duty through the city or otherwise enter Boston (Judges should review **Chapter One** regarding the possible character roles in Boston), the hair at the back of their necks stands on end and their stomachs knot up. They're being watched, and they know it. What once was a peaceful city in golden autumn becomes much more sinister as every building seems like it might be hiding an observer, and every crunch of a leaf makes the characters jump and spin, expecting to find someone behind them.

This air of paranoia begins once the characters leave Boston proper and the territory directly controlled by the Sons of Liberty. After a few blocks of this mystery, characters will notice a faint smell of blood with a Spot Check (DC 15) . Those who succeed on this check by more than 5 will spot a pack of four dogs standing in the distance down a street perpendicular to the one they are traveling on.

Unusually massive like many animals since the Revelation, the dogs appear to be mastiffs of a dull, mottled gray color. The entire pack stands eerily still and silent, observing the party. They will move to dodge any shots taken at them by the characters, and if pursued, they will turn and flee into the subway system of the city (See Appendix C for game statistics).

Characters attempting to follow them down should be made aware of the near-impenetrable dark that fills the tunnels. They will need a reliable source of light to avoid becoming immediately lost, and the Mastiffs will be almost impossible to follow.

Mood and Pacing – A Dark Tide Rising

The overall mood of **Act I** is two-fold: both introductory and foreboding. The players, should get a clear sense of the building tensions and problems facing Boston while they are being introduced to the colony, its residents, and its dangers.

Everything should seem new, but with an ominous feeling; residents are fearful or worried during introductions, buildings are heavily shadowed and looming at times; there are repeated glimpses of something (perhaps the Mastiffs of War, perhaps enemy soldiers, perhaps just wildlife) racing just through the edges of vision. Even the initial attacks by the enemy force and the scouting to determine their strength should feel like a build up of pressure before the release that is **Act II**.

Similarly, the pacing for this act should be one of escalation. Things start out slow and languid and build to a crescendo that announces **Act II**. Even the appearance of the Dogs is slow and the brief conflicts with enemy soldiers and scouting missions are long periods of waiting punctuated by brief, violent conflict. This can be hard to maintain, however. There is a thin line between "slow" and "glacial." Adjust the pace as you feel necessary.

They can quickly outpace the characters and their illumination and don't make any sound to follow once they are out of sight.

Once the characters continue on their way or the Mastiffs have escaped into the subways, the faint smell of blood will disappear and the uneasy feeling that began this scene will disappear. The Mastiffs have left.

The Downtrodden

Soon after their brief brush with the Mastiffs, the party (or any character acting as an advanced scout) will catch sight of a ragged column of people marching down the crumbling highway of I-90, the Mass Pike, heading towards the city. Apparently very lightly armed (only four rifles), about twenty men and a few women walk next to a car and a truck, both stuffed full of more women and a number of children. It is nearly impossible to get a good look at the passengers from a distance, but those walking are dressed simply in well-worn shoes and threadbare clothes. It is obvious that they have traveled for quite a while, their feet and the tires of the vehicles are caked with mud and the people walking are clearly exhausted. Some even pause to rest briefly, only to be forced to rush to catch up again.

Players may wish to report back to Lt. Col. Jefferson before making contact on their own or they may simply move ahead on their own initiative. Either way, the manner in which these travelers react when approached depends largely on how those approaching them act. Characters revealing themselves at a distance and walking up in an obviously friendly manner will be met with largely similar warmth. If the group is ambushed and held at gunpoint, they will return

that trust, forcing all parties to talk to each other over raised barrels. A warm and open welcome on the part of the characters will make the rest of the adventure run much more smoothly and easily, and Judges may want to play up the pitiful nature of the refugees in an attempt to generate sympathy for them. Lt. Col. Jefferson, if he is informed of their approach before contact is made, will have Philip Meer, Jefferson's right hand man, greet them. Ever cautious, Meer will approach the travelers with a strong escort and a hand extended in friendship. His guarded welcome is returned in kind, and after a few tense moments during introductions, everyone relaxes and the group is welcomed into the colony for further discussion. After all, manpower is needed in Boston.

The ragged travelers turn out to be refugees from what is left of New York, driven east by pressure from an organized and powerful military force. Lead by a woman named Rebecca Richards, they number thirty-one in all, including fourteen women and eight children between the ages of three and twelve. The children are especially rare and precious in ***The End*** and the attitude of the refugees clearly reflects this reality. Their exodus and dangers they have faced have obviously brought the refugees close together. Although they are overjoyed to find a friendly reception upon reaching their destination, most of them attempt to remain somewhat reserved from the Boston colonists, returning to "their own kind" after the initial joy of the welcoming.

Once introductions have been made and Lt. Col. Jefferson has heard their story, he will officially offer a place in the colony to the refugees, though Philip Meer or the characters may very well have done so already. The refugees are more than willing to take on the duties of any other member of the settlement and they readily accept. Jefferson asks the characters, since they were the first to encounter the refugees, to show the new members of the colony to an empty home near where the rest of the residents call their homes during autumn.

The Refugees (Typical Refugees;

The Refugees' Story

The refugees from New York are attempting to escape what they call a war. An ever-growing number of soldiers have moved into the ruined city of New York from the south during the past six months, taking control of any and all resources they could, from food stores to defunct power generators. Any (and as far as these refugees know, all) resistance was brutally crushed. The disorganized and isolated survivors of the city were completely unable to hold off the much better equipped and trained troops and most simply broke and fled, abandoning New York in hopes of finding a safer haven. Some ran north into upstate New York or Vermont while a few sought isolation and refuge on Long Island, but a significant number set out east, hoping to make it to Boston and the colony they had heard rumors of there.

Judges wishing to do so should feel free to embellish this brief tale with stories of atrocities suffered at the hands of the soldiers who now seem to hold New York or the trials the refugees had to face as they drove and walked their way through Connecticut and Massachusetts. An overland journey of that sort over several days was certainly not pleasant and war is always filled with tales of tragedy and sorrow.

see Appendix C) have run out of medical supplies and almost exhausted their food as well. Between all 31 refugees, they have only 4 Worn rifles and less than 50 rounds of ammunition. Rebecca Richards leads them.

War: The Attacks from Washington

As if to spoil the good fortune of welcoming the refugees into the colony, Boston is faced with another series of small, probing attacks almost immediately. As the characters are bringing the refugees to an open and suitable house, a number of other colony members run past them, shouting something about "There's another attack!" and "They're back again!" Anyone stopped for more information informs them that there has been another engagement with the enemy.

This sets up a brief but frantic period of desperate fighting as the colony desperately tries to defend itself, but without a clear idea of just what it is up against. Older women attempt to herd children into hidden shelters while able men and women grab whatever weapons they have and rush off to fight this new thrust by the enemy. Although the discipline instilled by Lt. Col. Jefferson quickly asserts itself and cuts through the air of disorganization, the confusion is never fully dispelled, as hard facts regarding just what kind of enemy force has appeared and just what kind of attack ensued remain few and far between.

Boston's relatively loose military structure serves it well. After only twenty minutes, Lt. Col. Jefferson reveals what information on the situation they have managed to confirm and arranges a force to deal with it, as well as making sure to distribute further troops elsewhere across the city on high alert. What is known is that one of the heavier scouting parties, a group of five men with radio equipment, was apparently ambushed by a hostile force to the south around Dorchester, where they were quickly pinned down inside an abandoned convenience store. The communications soldier was the first to fall, leaving his radio out of reach of the survivors, until they managed to push through briefly and retrieve it. It was that period of radio silence that informed the colony to the incident in the first place, and also what kept them from determining what exactly was going on.

Autumn is beautiful in New England

The events of *The Boston Massacre* are scripted as taking place over a period of a few weeks near the end of the year, beginning at the start of December as the chill of winter is beginning to take hold. The trees have all turned, painting the wilderness around the city in brilliant hues of brown, yellow, gold and red. Fallen leaves litter the ground even within the city, providing a dry and noisy blanket across the land. Snow is expected soon and the nights are cold.

This is, of course, easily changed. References to the season will be made throughout the adventure, especially in Chapter Four, but it does not rely upon them. Changing the season to spring or summer would make the situation somewhat easier on the Boston colonists, as those are the more temperate and forgiving times of the year. Conversely, setting this in the dead of winter would make it all the more deadly. The elements become even more an antagonist in their own right as starvation and exposure can, and likely will, sometimes take center stage in the struggle for survival.

Now that a clearer picture of the attack has emerged, Jefferson and his senior staff can conclude that the original scouting team, of which it is presumed that at most three members have survived, is being assaulted by an enemy force numbering perhaps twenty strong. In response, a powerful force of fifty men is sent to repel the enemy and, if possible, rescue the original scouts. Additionally, Jefferson distributes his remaining troops throughout the colony's territory, to ensure that this attack wasn't just the tip of the iceberg. As such, operations have one of two main motivations, either 1) to defeat the enemy the colony is aware of or; 2) to ensure the security of Boston's other borders. Characters may very likely want to involve themselves in the latter operation, radioing other scouting parties or taking part in the patrols themselves, and should the Judge agree, they are more than welcome to do so. It is assumed, however, that they are more driven to assist with the rescue force, and Judges are welcome to use direct orders from superiors to enforce such action if they need to. Boston, despite being a republic and defender of liberty, is still a military force at war – members do not have complete autonomy. Characters that directly disobey orders could be considered traitors, and in times of war traitors are often executed.

The Fight Scene

The scouting party is trapped in a convenience store approximately a half hour drive from central Boston, and the reactionary force sent by Jefferson races out there as quickly as they can. Several blocks from their target, the trucks are stopped and the soldiers disembark and march to the scene in an attempt to conceal their approach to some extent. Forward scouts are dispatched to get a reliable and detailed idea of the situation, both

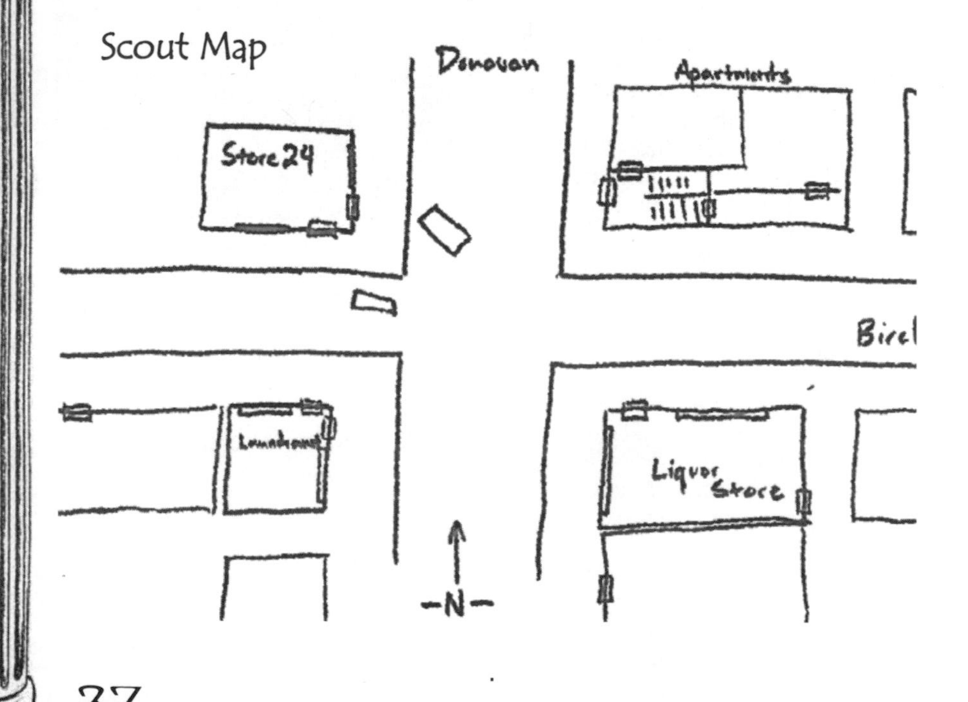

how much of the scouting team is left alive but, more importantly, where the enemy has entrenched itself.

As the Boston colonists already knew, the scouting team has holed itself up in a ruined convenience store, an old Store24 at the intersection of Birch Street and Donovan Street, abutting a large pile of rubble blocking off any rear exit. The invading force has simply splayed itself around the front of the building, waiting for the trapped soldiers to attempt to make a break for it. The buildings on the other three corners of the intersection that the ruined Store24 sits on have all been occupied and each contains approximately five enemy soldiers in it, as far as the scouts can determine.

After some deliberation, the commanding officers decide that the best option is the most cautious one. The Boston force takes up position mirroring their enemy's, watching all possible exits. The buildings are then set afire in an attempt to smoke out their targets, driving them into the open where they can be dealt with. Characters should be involved in the battle as part of a squad assigned to light one of the buildings on fire. They must be able to sneak up to it, remain undiscovered long enough to set the fire, and then escape. Many Move Silently, Spot and Listen checks will be essential, and if they are discovered, combat will ensue. Alternatively, they may want to be among the forces assigned to targeting any enemy troops that flee the buildings, requiring only attack rolls.

Those who find these tactics abhorrent can attempt to sway the decision of the commanding officer, an vibrant man by the name of Richard Patel (See Appendix C), though they face an uphill battle. After months of living in fear of the military might from the south, the soldiers are little inclined to mercy when facing the invading force. Instead, arguments about the possible danger of this smaller force making radio contact with whatever larger body sent them out or something similar are much more likely to be given serious consideration. Unless the players can suggest some sort of alternate plan of action to prevent that, however, it will only further convince the SOL soldiers that a swift and merciless assault is their only hope.

The Enemy Forces

The invading force has occupied three buildings, to the east, southeast, and south of the Store24 as well. The tallest building, to the east, is a three-story apartment complex of the sort scattered all around the city and a full six soldiers have settled into it, mostly at the top floor to provide a clear perch from which to watch the Store24. A liquor store once stood in the one-story building to the southeast. Four soldiers have made use of its open bay windows, now broken and covering the ground in bits of glass, to fire upon anyone out in the open through the intersection. To the south is a ruined laundromat and cleaning service where the rest of the enemy force, including its commander, is located. Along with five Rag-Tag soldiers and aids, the commander (add six hit points to the standard Rag-Tag soldier detailed in Appendix C) directs the miniature siege from the second floor, assisted by a unit of five further men who act as scouts and couriers between the three buildings. When the fighting starts, it is this last group that inflicts the most damage upon the SOL forces as they flee and shoot their way out before the final building is fully set aflame.

The Aftermath

If the tactic of burning the enemy out is employed, it is almost completely successful. Two of the three targeted buildings are easily caught afire and the people inside pose little threat as they run for their lives. The tallest building, to the east of the Store24, burns with amazing speed, and the six soldiers within it barely manage to run into the streets and fall beneath SOL's bullets before the entire structure collapses. The one-story building to the southeast of the scouting team's haven burns more slowly, but the enemy inside is smoked out and "disposed of" almost as readily. The final building to the south fares much better as the fire fails to truly catch. In the end, SOL soldiers are forced to use a precious grenade to open the front of it open and rush in, suffering virtually all of their casualties of the engagement in that battle.

When the dust settles and the shooting stops, the intersection of Birch and Donovan hosts seventeen enemy corpses and five SOL dead(this number should be adjusted for any dead party members of course), include the two scouts who originally fell. The SOL force further suffered four wounded, but only one severely so.

> **Capturing the Enemy**
>
> Experience Award. If the players are able to devise a manner in which to capture a Rag Tag soldier alive, they should receive an experience award equal to 3 times his CR. The Judge should not make this easy. This is a firefight after all, and characters should be forced to be clever. The Judge should also consider a small bonus if the characters make a good faith attempt to capture the enemy.

Scouting out the Enemy

While the battle has been won and the invaders have been defeated for the moment, the war continues on. Such is life within the Boston colony. Concerned that this latest incident presages a larger and more concerted attack upon the colony, and further worried that the news the refugees bring from New York is a sign of future troubles for his city, Lt. Col. Jefferson outlines a plan for an extensive deployment of scouting teams. Hoping to get a clear and detailed picture of the size and capabilities of the invasion force he may be facing, Jefferson puts the entire colony's resources behind this intelligence operation. Over the course of a few days, Susan Cominsky, Boston's best scout, brings the deep wilderness scouts she has trained back into the city. Using them as a foundation, Jefferson restructures a significant portion of his force into a number of small, mobile teams.

These teams of five men and women are filtered out into the terrain around the city and each is put under the direct command of one of Cominsky's scouts. Each of those scouts directly coordinates between the teams in a broad area, serving as a field commander of sorts during this operation. Cominsky and Jefferson personally oversee this network, while Meer takes on the task of reinforcing the colony's defenses throughout their territory. Each scout team is given strict orders to return with information, not to attempt to enter combat with anyone they may encounter. When they do come across hostile soldiers, the teams are to temporarily withdraw (after determining the force's strength) and report in, and then probe further. The goal of the operation is to gather as much information about the enemy as possible while concealing this heightened sense of awareness for as long as possible. Overconfidence has been the failing of Boston's opponent for quite a while, and Jefferson hopes it will continue to remain so.

Specific character assignments may vary a great deal, depending on character concepts and the pace of the story. Boston is in desperate need of a clear grasp of what it is fighting against, and disperses much of its fighting force throughout the city and the outlying area in an attempt to get that. Relatively low-ranking characters will be given standard patrol duties, ordered simply to sweep through a section of the city to find out the enemy is or was there. More experienced characters or those with specialized skills will be called on for more precise missions, from more extended scouting missions to following up on leads regarding possible emplacements of enemy forces possibly uncovered by the more routine patrols. Some short samples are provided as ideas that Judges can use to build brief scouting encounters.

On Patrol – The characters are simply assigned to patrol a several block area, determine if the enemy is or has been through it, and report their findings back to their superior. Numerous Spot and Listen checks (with the DC usually 15, but varying depending on the skill of the enemy forces present, if any) will be required to find any hidden or unseen enemy troops. Search rolls (DC 15-20) are required to find traces of troops that have moved through the area, and Tracking (DC 17-25) can be used to determine where the came from and where they were likely headed. If the Judge has not specifically decided whether or not the enemy is present, there is a 30% chance they are. Successful Completion Experience Award: 1 CR equivalent per hidden enemy revealed or meaningful trace recovered.

Confirming a Supply Depot – Near the Charles River, just to the west of Boston proper, a large moving van has been parked in an empty lot to make it easily accessible to all colonists and

stuffed full of supplies, including blankets, clothing and weapons. The characters have been assigned, likely while en route to another mission, to locate and confirm its safety. It is a simple matter to locate the van and confirm the supplies therein (Search check, DC 10). However, if the Judge has not decided whether the enemy has discovered this depot already, there is a 60% chance they have. The Washington forces can find large yellow trucks just as easily as a Boston colonist. Successful Completion Experience Award: 2 CR equivalent for locating and secure the van, 4 CR is they party recovers it undamaged from enemy forces that control it.

Investigating a Report on the Enemy– Another group on patrol has reported that they found evidence that some of the invading force passed through their patrol area and may still

A Guided Tour of the City of Boston

These scenes serve something of a dual purpose. Aside from simply providing information on the size and nature of the enemy, these scouting missions provide the Judge with the opportunity to familiarize his players with the city the game is set in. In addition, they provide a non-linear format in which the Judge can slowly reveal important details about this adventure. While the characters may know the city well, it is very unlikely that the players will. Giving them something of a guided tour in **Act I** will allow them to make use of some city knowledge during the larger pitched battles in **Act II**, giving them a feeling of really being able to take an active hand in the defense of their character's homes. Judges should think on where they want much of the action in the second act and then ensure that the players have the opportunity to explore that area here.

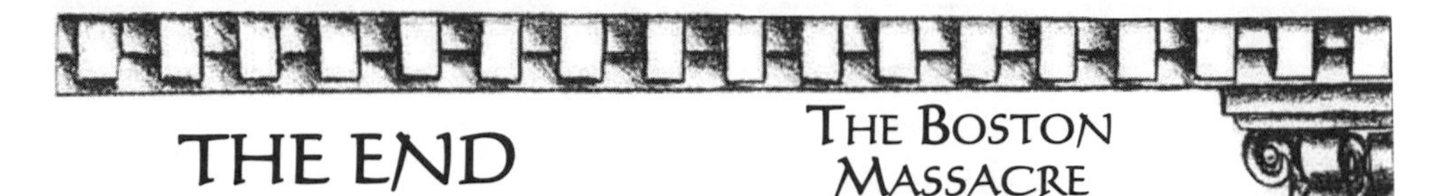

Just When Things Couldn't Get Worse

During these scouting operations, very perceptive characters (Spot: DC 20) will notice another colonist by the name of Keith Lyons suffering from a severe cough and seeming weaker than usual. A somewhat proud man, he refuses any assistance and assures any who inquire that he's fine, "It's just a little thing, we got bigger problems now." Lyons' ailment is indeed minor in the beginning, but has become something significantly more debilitating by the time the size of the invading force becomes clear. It escalates to the point where he is coughing up blood and is barely able to walk straight (see below in **Act II**). At breakfast one day, Lyons collapses with extreme fever and exhaustion. The limited medical staff of the colony is at a complete loss to diagnose, let alone treat, this new disease.

Lyon's Plague ("Creeping Death")

Symptoms: After an incubation period of a few days to a few weeks, depending on the victim, the disease first causes exhaustion and other symptoms common to many diseases, such as clogged mucus membranes, headaches, mild fever, loss of appetite or gastro-intestinal difficulties. Once that stage has passed, however, the disease quickly escalates, first causing wracking coughing fits and then beginning to fill the lungs with blood. Eventually the victim drowns in their own blood.

Vectors: It is not entirely clear how the plague is transmitted, although a great deal of evidence points towards bodily contact, especially exposure to infected fluids such as blood or saliva.

Treatment: Whether or not Lyon's Plague is curable or even treatable is still unclear, but a few different concoctions of various plant extracts seem to have had some success in curbing the suffering of infected patients, at least, and some rumors exist of survivors.

Game Data: Judges should adjust this disease as needed. Players exposed to Lyon's Plague (and the Judge shall decide how such exposure occurs) should make a Fortitude Save (DC 18) to avoid developing the disease. Characters with Concoction or Treat Illness can make a check (DC 25) to successfully make a poultice, but this may only be attempted once per attempting character.

Just as their mortal enemies move to close in on Boston, a more insidious enemy has begun to stalk them.

be nearby. The characters are sent in to confirm this and deal with the enemy, if they find them to be small enough. There is a 75% chance that the report is accurate, but only a 50% chance that the enemy force has more than 2d6 Rag-Tag soldiers in it (See Appendix C). They have established a temporary camp within a small café between two decrepit clothing stores in a shopping district (DC 17 Search check) and are resting when the characters find them (they will be surprised it attacked). Successful Completion Experience Award: 2 CR equivalent bonus for surviving.

Exploring Southern Roads – The characters are sent south on I-95 (towards Providence, RI) to see how far north Washington's Rag Tag's have traveled. Unless they can scavenge some gasoline themselves (Scavenge check, DC 20), they are given bicycles with which to make the trip. The road itself has weathered The End relatively well and makes for smooth, easy travel. After a few hours, about 10 miles beyond the metropolitan area, characters can start making Spot checks (DC 17) every mile to notice signs of the invader's advance to that point. Characters who actually stop and Search only face a DC of 12 or the same roll, and can make the check every quarter of a mile. There is a 25% chance that they may face a similar scouting party from the enemy during their travels. Successful Completion Experience Award: 5 CR equivalent bonus for identifying the edge of the Rag-Tag advance.

Each squad is more heavily armed than usual for Boston defenders, but thankfully they do not engage the enemy further. What they discover over the course of a few weeks, however, is far from heartening. A massive force (estimates can only place it between six or seven hundred soldiers) lies to the south of Boston, beyond the suburbs in Quincy. Worse, it seems very well supplied and better trained than the previous forces Boston has faced. Scouts report quality rifles and shotguns being standard issue and some form of armor, even riot armor, as disturbingly common. A handful of converted riot vehicles are also in evidence, with New York or Washington, D.C. license plates (and department logos on those not repainted), confirming suspicions regarding the invader's origins.

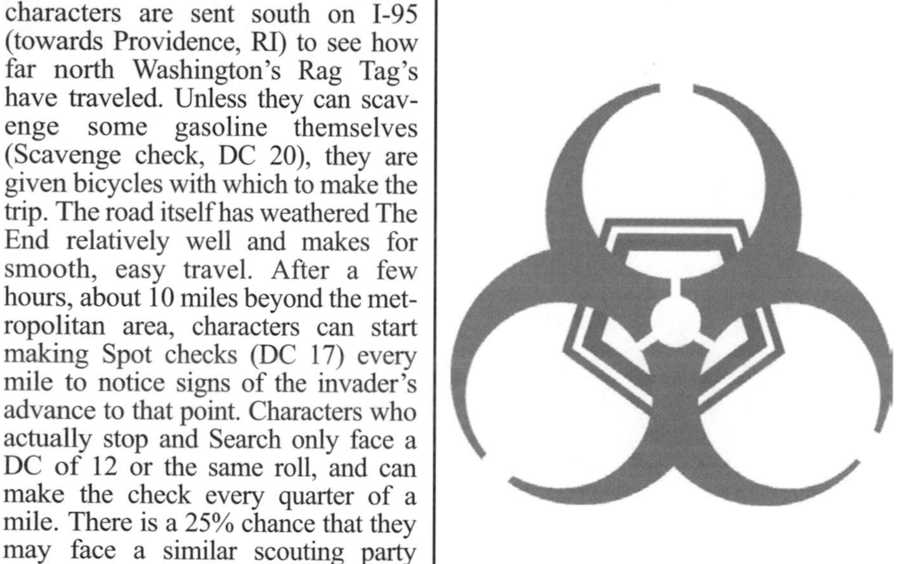

ACT II: THE SMACK-DOWN

The Mastiffs of War

Shortly after dawn, as they return from one of the last scouting sweeps, the characters again fall under the eerie atmosphere that marked the beginning of these trials. Just as they are about to return to the territory solidly held by the Sons of Liberty, their hackles rise and they get the undeniable feeling that *something* is watching them as the scent of fresh blood wafts on thc brcczc. Doing littlc to conceal their presence this time, the Mastiffs are easy to spot, requiring only an easy Spot check (DC 10) to locate.

Looking down upon the characters from atop several old cars in a ruined dealership, the four Mastiffs spend only a moment to take stock of them before turning and trotting away through the maze of abandoned cars. Attempts to follow or stop the Mastiffs are fruitless, as if they had simply faded into thin air. Again, the pack makes no noise, even when they jump from the cars, and the scent of blood disappears soon after they do.

Lyon's Plague: The First Death from the Disease

After providing a full report to Jefferson and meeting with the scout commanding them, the characters have a chance to enjoy a late breakfast, along with the other colony members not out scouting or on patrol. After two weeks of near-constant deployment around the city, the opportunity to sit down and relax with some real food should seem like heaven. The rest of the colonists at the meal are somewhat pensive, but the lack of activity on the part of the invasion force has heartened most of them, and the morning is the most hopeful and pleasant of the last few weeks.

Keith Lyons is also at the breakfast, still suffering from his cough, which has very obviously gotten much worse. He is coughing almost constantly now. In fact, characters succeeding on a very difficult Spot check (DC 25) will realize that Keith Lyons' handkerchief is stained with blood and he is obviously in extreme

Mood and Pacing – A Desperate Struggle

In contrast to the previous act's slow and somewhat leisurely pace, allowing the players a chance to be introduced and adjust to the setting, the second act is much more rushed, almost frantic. Things begin to hit the fan as Washington mounts another invasion upon the city and while an unknown new disease makes itself known with deadly results. The mood is one of action and danger, and the pacing should emphasize that. Characters should be rushed around from one event to another- witnessing the devastating effects of this new disease and participating in one brief, deadly fight after another until everything suddenly just *stops* and the colony nearly trips over itself before getting a chance to catch its breath.

Pressure is the key here. The pressure from the hostile army to the south and from the disease in their midst is the impetus that drives the colony, and thus the characters, to mount the expedition constituting **Act III** as well as lending **Act IV** much of its haste and urgency.

pain. Despite being wracked by fits of uncontrollable coughing and unable to conceal the blood if confronted about it, he will insist that he is okay and tries to get something to eat. Almost immediately, however, he completely collapses, sending food flying everywhere as he falls onto the table holding bread and soup.

Keith Lyons has a frightening fever (in excess of 110 degrees F) and Jaime Dahlke and his staff are baffled by the cause and can only provide general treatment, which is completely ineffective. The doctor cannot make any sort of prognosis and readily admits that he has no idea how long it will take for Keith Lyons to recover, or even if he will survive at all. The best he is able to do is attempt to reduce the pain and fever a bit. Jaime Dahlke does say that he fears the worst, and he is tragically proven correct when Lyons regains consciousness later that night only to continue coughing until blood is nearly constantly pouring from his mouth and he dies in agony.

Washington Strikes Again

Lyon's death is far from the only tragedy to strike Boston that night as the invaders to the south begin moving again, striking under the cover of darkness. The colony remains on alert, so the attack does not take them completely by surprise. The enemy forces seemed to have split into three columns in an attempt to spread out their strength and trap Boston within the three-pronged attack. One force circles around and heads into the city from the west while the two others both rush north into the city. Even worse, the attacks make it clear that this conflict may not end as well for Boston as previous ones have. The invaders seem to have learned from past mistakes and much of their overconfidence has evaporated. Over the course of a few days, three major battles define the conflict. To the south, *Jamaica Plain* becomes a warzone as two armies stare over their gun at each other. To the west, the *Brighton police station* plays host to the last stand of a vastly outnumbered Boston force under siege in one of the colony's major supply depots. Finally, to the east, Jefferson himself leads a force to hold a strategically *important bridge*. The characters may become involved in any or all of these conflicts. Perhaps they are among the defenders in Brighton, hoping for salvation to arrive in time, or perhaps they act like the cavalry, traveling all over the city as needed.

Boston's Tactics

Relying upon the methods they have used to great effect so far, the Sons of Liberty engage in a vicious guerrilla battle with the enemy. SOL soldiers quickly separate into small squads and scatter themselves across the enemy's path to make devastating ambushes. A squad will typically wait in a building they expect the enemy to march past and open fire once the front line has passed. Perched on the rooftops of these buildings, a number of squads are able to inflict heavy casualties before being killed themselves or forced to retreat.

Other squads, however, take more inventive paths. Some use the colony's limited supplies of explosive in attempts to topple buildings. If brought town into a street before the enemy arrives, rubble can be used to try to herd them somewhere more desirable, usually towards other squads who have set up powerful killing fields. Other times the buildings are demolished while the enemy passes by them, less in the hope that they will be crushed than in an attempt to divide the force into smaller and more manageable units. One squad will destroy a building and cut a section of the enemy force off from its fellows and other squads will step in to "clean up" the area.

In defense of their home and their lives, the Sons of Liberty use almost every method they can think of to gain even the smallest advantage. Homemade bombs hidden in cars or rubble, rigging building facades to collapse after placing enticing food or equipment inside or even just rolling cars down hills in the general direction of the enemy; Boston makes use of everything at its disposal.

Despite this desperate ingenuity, the colony fares poorly under this new assault. Sheer weight of numbers can be a powerful force, and the invaders have shown themselves more than willing to use their strength in that manner. Worse, as the fight wears on, it becomes more and more obvious that the enemy is learning from its previous failures. Characters can make a real and tangible difference here. Cunning strategies and devastating ploys will tip the balance in favor of the defenders.

Short Sample Encounters

Judges looking to add some additional encounters to make this chapter really feel like a short war can add a number of other missions or surprises to their game. A few are suggested here as seeds to give inspiration. As with the rest of the adventure, feel free to add more to adapt the game as needed or desired. Soldiers from both sides can be drawn from Appendix C.

Demolition – In order to block possible avenues of attack from the south and the east, Jefferson has ordered the destruction of some of Boston's remaining sky scrapers and other buildings over four stories. Characters may be sent to protect the demolition teams, or if they have the necessary skills themselves, sent as part of the teams. Properly setting up the explosives requires 4 Disable Device checks (DC 17 for each). Failure on more than one will mean that the building was destroyed, but only partially blocking the intended road, if at all. Failing even one roll by more than 10 will result in someone being caught in a direct explosion or destroying the building prematurely and trapping someone inside. Perhaps both if the roll is failed by more than 15.

Ambush – Having stumbled across a patrol of 2d4+4 enemy soldiers (Spot or Listen check, DC 15) without being seen themselves (Move Silently check, DC 15), the characters have the opportunity to place an ambush for the enemy squad, gaining full surprise when they open fire and catch them unawares. Characters should be careful, however, that they do not bite off more than they can chew and attack a force they cannot defeat, unless they have an assured route of escape handy.

Supplies – Proper distribution of the colony's meager supplies is essential to surviving this conflict, and the characters are given the responsibility of ferrying a number of recently refurbished rifles and pistols (12 Worn rifles, 20 Worn pistols) as well as 500 rounds of standard ammunition from one of the supply depots in Brighton to the soldiers in Jamaica Plain. Unfortunately, they run afoul of an enemy strike force, including a sniper, along the way. They will need to either escape or somehow defeat this well-trained enemy force if they are going to be able to deliver their much needed supplies to the front.

Completion experience awards may be awarded by the Judge at their discretion but should not exceed 3 CR equivalent.

THE END

Jamaica Plain (2:41 a.m)

During the night, the largest hostile force heads up toward the center of the city, trying to push forward as far as it can. Still maintaining something of a column formation, nearly five hundred enemy soldiers march on Boston, passing through and overwhelming the first sentries far from the city, but not before the sentries are able to get the word out and alert the colony. Jefferson quickly rouses his Sons of Liberty to defend their homes and fully half of his force almost manages to halt the invading force during bitter house-to-house fighting.

From the several hours from the first assault to the breaking of dawn when the Rag-Tag's column unexpectedly entrenches itself in the buildings it managed to reach, this engagement is a running battle. The enemy force seems to advance inexorably, although SOL squads continue to harry it the entire way. As the main column continues forward, smaller units of invaders (2-6 Rag-Tag soldiers; see Appendix C) are dispatched to neutralize the SOL guerrillas. Though they rarely return, the small Rag-Tag units do serve to occupy the SOL, allowing the main Biker Army force to continue on unhindered.

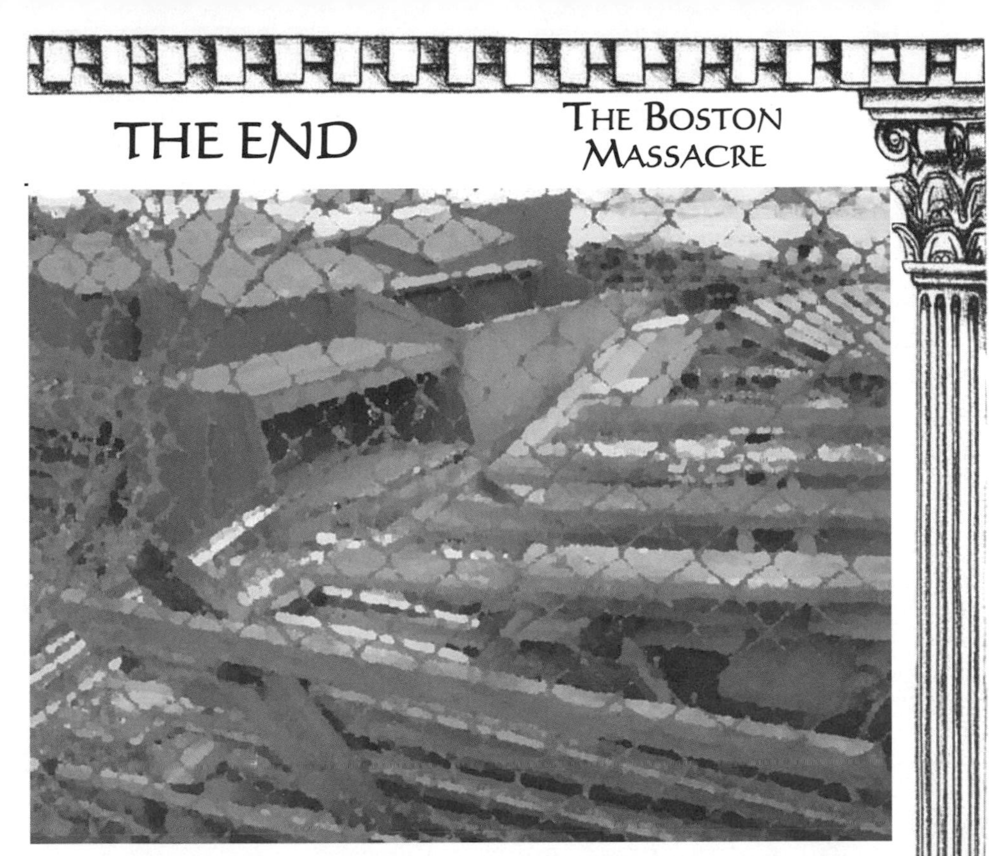

Jamaica Plain is a largely residential area, filled with small streets and many tightly-packed three or four story homes. Boston's familiarity with the area is its only advantage, providing it with many opportunities for ambushes and traps. The invaders' strategy, on the other hand, is to form a broad front and walk forward, capturing one side of a street, and then crossing to capture the next. From the initial engagement to the point where the Washington force stopped, it managed to advance across and secure 6 blocks. Characters may be assigned as part of a guerilla squad, sneaking around (Move Silently, DC 15+) to flank the enemy and attack from behind in an attempt to divert their attention. After the first few hours, however, this tactic becomes more and more dangerous as Washington sends out its own squads in response. Or the characters may take up a defensive position within a building on one of the Jamaica Plain streets. Jefferson is more than aware of the size of the force advancing upon his position, however, and has made it clear that lives are more important than buildings at this point.

When dawn arrives, however, to the astonishment of the Sons, the army stops and filters into the buildings around it, taking cover, as if bunkering down for a heavy assault. Baffled, the defenders are unable to do much other than entrench themselves and wait.

The Battle of Brighton (6:20 a.m.)

While the larger force makes a spectacle of marching towards Boston, another enemy division makes its way west to loop around and attack the colony from another direction. The SOL's attention distracted by the battle to the south, this second attack manages to catch the SOL defenders by surprise and they are quickly routed until they regroup much deeper within the city.

Unlike the fighting that raged

through Jamaica Plain before dawn, this force does not march stubbornly onward. Instead the smaller division, one hundred strong, seems to have a string of very distinct targets, rushing from one of Boston's western supply depots to another. Almost as worrying as this loss of valuable resources is the certainty with which the enemy moves to each hidden location. It is obvious that someone has leaked the information.

Judas

If the characters discover that Joseph Meehan is a traitor and provide proof, they should be awarded experience equivalent to overcoming a CR 6 opponent. If they merely kill or remove Joseph Meehan, they may receive a CR 3 equivalent bonus, but unless they prove he was a traitor, the SOL could be very upset...

The defenders make their final stand at the Brighton police station, only a couple hours walk from the center of Boston. The largest of the supply caches in the area, the police station was usually visited by colonists and travelers heading west or north out of the city. Now, fifty SOL soldiers have barricaded themselves within to defend the important store of food, fuel and ammunition from nearly four times their number. Surrounded by a parking lot and a broad lawn leading to two or three story homes and business, the station is a solid and defensible location. That was why it was chosen as a depot in the first place. Despite its security, however, it can only hold out for so long before it is simply overwhelmed. Unless the "cavalry" arrive or those inside are able to mount a successful counter-attack, Boston will lose the west of the metropolitan area, and all the supplies they have stored there, to the enemy.

The Brighton police station is rel-

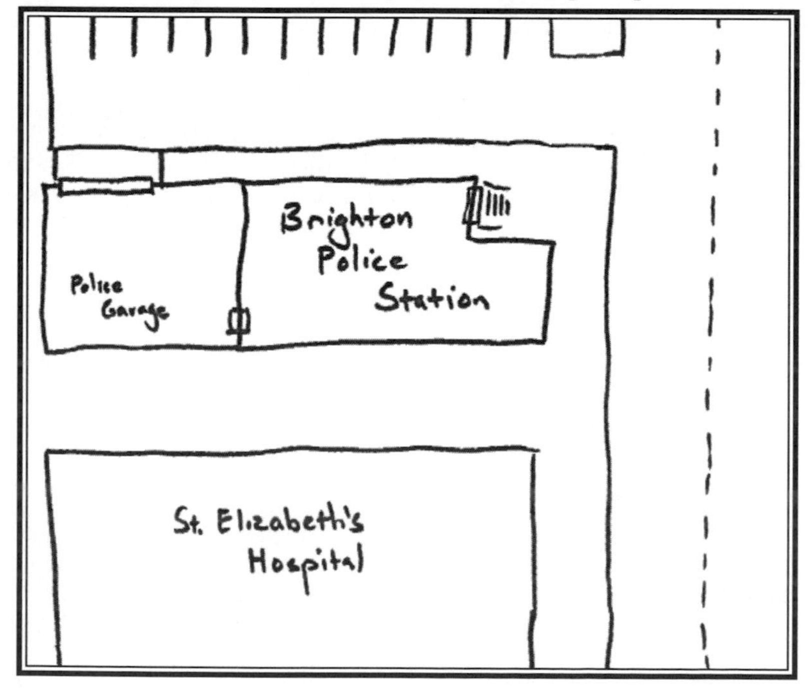

atively isolated with a broad lawn on one side and a parking lot on the other. Beyond the parking lot are a number of several story residential homes. The thoroughly looted remains of St. Elizabeth's Hospital lie opposite the lawn, and just to the east is Brighton center, with all of the commercial buildings that would be associated with it. The husks of restaurants, liquor stores and convenience stores stretch down the road away from the station itself. The defenders are able to get one or two shots at anyone who simply rushes at them, which is usually enough. Before long, however, the Rag-Tags wise up and sit in for a waiting game of their own. Eventually the Rag-Tags procure some disposable vehicles, scavenging abandoned cars from the area and proceed to attempt to crash into the police station, using the car as a shield of sorts. Some expert shooting or heavier weaponry than simple rifles will be needed to prevent this from succeeding, forcing the colonists into close-quarters combat.

Anyone attempting to rescue those trapped within the station has a few options. If they are intent only on a rescue, they need only clear a path for escape and cover the SOL retreat. Protecting the supply depot is a much more difficult task (CR 6 award), however, requiring either a force larger than the enemy's or some innovative tactics. Somehow convincing the Washington force that they are facing a larger number reinforcements may work, as would quietly flanking them. Truly desperate characters may even attempt to use the same tactics as in the previous chapter and try to burn their opponents out. Arson will only work on some locations, however, as the fire is unlikely to travel from the taller residential area to the commercial district without further coaxing.

Blood on the River (12:49)

The second day of the assault begins as poorly as the first, the attack on two fronts becomes three as the remainder of the invasion force attacks from the southeast along the waterfront around midday. With Boston's forces already divided, this third column does not need to bother with stealthy ploys of any sort. Simply marching up toward the skyscrapers still standing in the center of Boston, this collection of approximately four hundred soldiers threatens to advance upon the very heart of the colony itself.

Jefferson himself takes command of the resistance against the third Biker Army column, allowing the enemy to advance with minimal resistance until they reach the bridges crossing the Fort Point Channel. There he uses the bridges as a bottleneck to stop the advancing army dead in its tracks with minimal exposure of his own troops. More of the colony precious explosives are mounted on the bridges themselves, to deny their use to the enemy as a last resort if the bridges cannot be held.. This battle is much more static than many of the others during this conflict, as both sides have concentrated on one specific point of strategic importance. Characters are likely to be involved in defense simply to attack the Washington army as it advances over the bridge. The bridge confines the enemy's advance, creating something of a killing field. The opening attacks of this battle are simply slaughters.

This ploy will only work for a limited time, as the channel is not exceptionally wide. The hostile army can take a detour of a bit more than an hour to skirt around it. That would, however, bring them close to the first column of invaders that assault the city the previous morning, allowing the colony to unite the two fronts and recombine its forces.

The third invasion force is far from content to surrender the bridges to Boston without a challenge. Behind a façade of overconfidence and impotent attempts to batter through the defenders, small sabotage units are being sent across the channel. At first they are sent around the channel, using some of the enemy's riot vehicles and motorcycles to cover the distance quickly. Later troops attempt to swim over the channel. These flanking tactics severely weaken the already small defending force. Without some intervention, Jefferson will be unable to destroy the bridges

The Refugees During the Crisis

During these deadly battles with the Washington forces, the refugees do what they can to help the colony. Their able-bodied men and women are given weapons and fight bravely. The young ferry supplies and news around, acting as gophers. The elderly spend much of their time tending to the wounded and preparing food and supplies for those in the thick of the fighting. That is to say, they work to defend Boston just the same as any long-time resident.

Judges may wish to emphasize their presence to further assist the story. The "Refuse" may commit acts of amazing bravery, sacrificing themselves for the greater good. They may rush in as cavalry to save the characters just when they needed help the most. They may provide tender care for a wounded character.

No matter what they do, the more connections with the characters the Judge can forge, the less forced the end of the act will seem. Similarly, the more useful and noble the refugees can be made to seem, the more troubling the decisions of **Act IV** will be.

before the Washington force moves across them. Characters may volunteer to seek out and destroy these sabotage units, fighting a much more fluid battle in the neighborhoods around the bridge. They may also volunteer to protect the explosives on the bridge from being disarmed, or they could even attempt to set them off. If they can convince Jefferson that they will be able to actually destroy the bridges, he will change his strategy slightly, withdrawing to lure the enemy onto and over the bridge. After some of the troops have crossed over, the characters need to destroy the bridge, eliminating a large number of soldiers already on the bridge and, more importantly, splitting the enemy force in to two smaller pieces, which are much more easily dealt with by the beleaguered Boston colonists.

The Eye of the Storm (5:31 p.m.)

Just as Jefferson's forces on the bridges break, and the central enemy column gears up to continue its advance, Boston is blessed with what at first seems like a miracle. For no apparent reason, each of the enemy columns withdraw just as their victory seemed imminent. The two columns to the south halt their advance and retrace their path out of the city while the one to the west does the same, pausing only to make sure that each of the supply caches it overran are fully looted and set aflame. Each force engages only those weary Boston defenders that follow them.

As their fellows rejoice at their change of fortune, however mysterious, the characters catch scent of that now disturbingly familiar smell of blood, even over that of the carnage around them. Investigation reveals what they fear, the mysterious mastiffs. This time, however, the pack of massive canines seems unconcerned with them, instead focusing on a corpse they have found. Sniffing and pawing at the body amid the buzzing of flies, one of them turns to watch the characters as the stumble across the scene. Its gaze remains on them as its fellows silently pad deeper into the alley and around a corner before it turns and follows.

The body itself turns out to be that of one of the refugee women, Roberta Kaplan. Her mouth is caked with dried blood and it looks like she had been coughing or vomiting it over her forearms as well, just as Keith Lyons did when he died. From the state the body, it is clear that she has been dead for a while. After a brief examination, Jaime Dahlke can confirm that whatever claimed Lyons seems to have killed her as well. Indeed, she seems to have died the day before he did.

Prisoners and Information

Should the characters have the opportunity to capture enemy soldiers and make use of it, there is some further information about the enemy they can discover, though the prisoners are extraordinarily difficult to interrogate. The are neither well disciplines or loyal, but remain absolutely terrified of something, most refuse to say anything at all, except perhaps pleading to be released. If the characters can succeed on a DC 20 Intimidation check, they can crack one of the prisoners, getting him to reveal what he knows. Doing so, however, quickly drives the man insane and he is only able to provide vague information. Any of them can confirm that the original invasion force has its home in Washington, D.C., but they did draw a number of converts and conscripts from New York, however, as well as supplementing their supplies with equipment looted from the ruins of the Big Apple in varying conditions. Those from Washington itself can also tell disturbing tales of crowds venerating a dark, mist shrouded man and an enormous pentagon fortress. Even on the march, the commanding officers have still enforced this worship of the "Bloodied Father" or "the Wrathful."

Washington's intent for Boston, and likely other cities, was made clear in New York. After destroying what little resistance there was, the army began converting the populace, enlisting able-bodied men into the military and enforcing their violent religion upon everyone within their dominion. Washington is building an empire, one baptized in blood and death.

A Council Meeting in Boston (9:57 p.m.)

Jefferson makes full use of the short reprieve his colony has been granted, immediately calling the leaders of the colony together to decide on a course of action. Just as Jefferson calls the meeting, the first flakes of winter snow begin to fall. The sudden withdrawal by the Washington forces would seem to signal a willingness to let the colony be until winter passes and spring comes again. Surviving the brutal winter is not going to be easy, however, with the massive loss of supplies and manpower the colony suffered over the course of only two days.

Calling upon Susan Cominsky, Philip Meer and Rebecca Richards, Jefferson entertains plans to survive the coming winter. It is clear that something needs to be done. Even if it is possible to last the season with the supplies the colony has at the moment, the colony will be in no shape to put up any sort of resistance against the Washington force come spring. Replenishing their stores is of paramount importance.

Through the course of the meeting Meer half-heartedly suggests that Cape Cod or Rhode Island may hold untouched stores. However, the invasion force sitting squarely between Boston and those locations makes any such expedition over land impossible and none of the colony's members are good enough seamen to travel by boat around the Cape. Cominsky confirms the unfortunate truth that there are no major unspoiled stores within easy reach of the colony, and hope seems lost. Rebecca Richards, however, reminds Jefferson and his advisors of her journey from New York with her fellow refugees. They passed through Connecticut and some of western Massachusetts, but did not encounter any settlements or colonies. With no one to thoroughly plunder it, the cities between Boston and New York, such as Hartford, Connecticut, should have enough to supply the colony and keep it strong until spring. Assuming those stores can be gotten past Washington's encampment, of course.

Worried that the enemy may launch another offensive before the grip of winter fully sets in, Jefferson realizes that he cannot spare a large number of soldiers from his already weakened defense. Ultimately he decides that four teams will be sent out in different directions. Two will be sent north, into New Hampshire and Maine, to scavenge and hunt as best they can. Two others will be sent west, one into western Massachusetts and the other will later turn southward into Connecticut, following some of the route the refugees took to reach Boston. Three refugees will accompany the last group to act as guides and all four teams will be given the best equipment that the colony can spare (Good condition), including trucks with large loads of fuel and plenty of ammunition. Recovering food is of the highest priority, along with further ammunition, medical supplies, and weaponry. Beyond that, Jefferson asks each party to try to retrieve as much information as possible. Boston is a colony in desperate straits and truly in need of any ally it can find. More hands and strong backs can serve just as well as bread come spring.

The characters are nominated to form the group to head into Connecticut with the refugees. Due to their history with the group, though they can decline if they so desire. If that is the case, the Judge will have to restructure the entirety of **Act III** to reflect that the characters did not accompany the refugees and stumble across the revelations that define much of the conflict in **Act IV**.

ACT III: THE PAUSE THAT REFRESHES

The Mastiffs of War

An early snowfall marks their departure from Boston as the four teams leave under an almost picturesque scene of light flakes drifting in the cold. Misty breath fills the air instead of words, but the silence speaks clearly. The survival of the colony depends upon these four parties returning with the supplies necessary not only to endure the winter but to emerge in spring strong enough to resist the pressures of Washington, D.C. Trucks are loaded up with fuel and supplies in a somber mood and that hardly lifts as everyone clambers in their vehicles and drive out of the haven of Boston.

Their departure is far from unnoticed, however. Extremely perceptive characters (Spot check (DC 25)) will recognize the scent of blood upon the air again as they leave and all four Mastiffs watch the entire caravan pass them on the highway. Impassive and motionless, the quartet of beasts simply observes, radiating an almost palpable aura of patience.

Mood and Pacing – A Moment to Consider

This act returns to the slower pacing of the first act, but with a much tenser air. This expedition is important, and its success or failure may well determine whether the colony of Boston stands or falls. Time is of the essence, but the act shifts the story's focus from conflicting military powers to the struggle to survive in the wilderness. An inhuman antagonist makes for a much different pace of events. While starvation and exposure can kill just as easily as a bullet, they do so on a much longer time frame. What is more, they are not something that can ever be permanently defeated. Hunger cannot be killed nor can the weather be conquered, they can only be resisted.

Act III is a period of relative calm in which the players can attempt to piece together what is going on around them while they struggle with the task of survival. As such, it should be a much more contemplative period, punctuated by tense moments clearly illustrating the dangers of the wilds.

A Further Note

It is worth mentioning that **Act III** is structured much differently from the other Acts. It is very loose. Even more than the other chapters of this adventure, this act can be tailored and modified to suit the Judge's needs. Indeed it *must* be. Few concrete encounters are detailed. Instead, several suggestions and guidelines are provided. Individual Judges must decide what, if any, encounters with the power of nature the characters must face. People can drive to Connecticut and back in scarcely an afternoon today, so skipping over the journey and simply focusing on the destination or the encounters with the motorcycle gangs may be the best course for some groups. A longer, detailed trek and struggle against the frontier may appeal to others. The refrain that the Judge should use his own discretion is again applicable, but deserves special mention here, as the chapter cannot simply be followed from start to finish without some embellishment.

Traveling in the Wilderness

Not far from the city, the four groups separate and disperse, heading toward their destinations. Two turn to the northern roads and one continues west while the characters turn southward, towards Connecticut. Each is seeking out supplies and provisions, but hoping for more. Each carries the hope that the metropolitan areas that they will encounter have not been completely looted or fallen to the Blues, but they also desperately hope to find a possible link to another colony. Reinforcements, sheer manpower, could serve Boston as well as food, fuel or bullets now.

The wilderness after the Rapture is not the domain of man. To call it forbidding would not properly describe it, as it is lush and fruitful, but very much *not* Man's land. If tested, this reality will be proven with an impassionate and implacable finality. Traveling through this hostile wilderness in ***The End*** is not a light undertaking, and not simply out of the fear of encountering equally desperate and dangerous survivors out beyond the reach of any assistance (see the Encounter Table on page 16). See the Book of Lamentations in ***The End*** for information on some of the encounters the characters may stumble into. Treks through the wilderness face nature itself in its many splendored and terrifying forms. Food, fuel and ammunition, the staples of survival for the Meek, are even more limited than usual, as they must be carried along. Shelter must be taken where possible. Weather is completely beyond anyone's control and can be a savior and a destroyer in turn. Landslides, roadblocks, animal attacks, blizzards, torrential rainstorms and even perhaps the odd traveler can become trials even more dangerous than the pitched battles the character fought back home in

Equipment

Each departing party is provided roughly similar equipment and provision. Two pickup trucks with two spare tires, three days worth of fuel and a similar volume of food and water as well as simple hunting rifles and 400 rounds are given to both. Medical supplies are limited, consisting of a single first aid kit, as the colony has a much more present need for them. Finally, each team is given a single radio to keep in touch with the colony, if the need arises. All equipment is in "good" condition.

The players are free to request further supplies, and there is a chance that they will get any reasonable requests. Boston's resources, however, are somewhat limited, and an item's potential utility with one of the scouting parties must be weight against its real utility within the colony itself. Any advanced items will be in Worn condition (See Book of Lamentations in ***The End***, pages 202-204), others should be in Good condition. Jefferson knows that the colony will needs medical supplies and advanced weaponry, but the scouting teams may or may not, so those are kept within Boston. Judges are urged to use their discretion.

Boston.

In the modern era, traveling from Boston all the way to New York City is simply a matter of a few hours by car. Well-maintained highways allow cars to journey across the land quickly and efficiently, but times have changed. Both the Blues and simply nature itself have taken their toll on the roadways of America, and New England is far from well-traveled territory. Most of the roads and highways are in advanced stages of decay ("Worn" equivalent or worse). Most are simply rough, riddled with potholes and enormous cracks, making rides bumpy and severely limiting maximum speeds, but some have disappeared almost entirely, crumbling to black dust or split apart by the voracious advance of the forest. Perhaps more troublesome than this decay is the unpredictability with which roadways are affected. Recovered road maps are very detailed, but it is virtually impossible to predict which roads will turn out to be impassable. Exploration involves substantial amounts of turning and backtracking when an otherwise passable road turns out to be obstructed or destroyed. Under these frustrating and difficult conditions, characters can expect to take a day, or even more, to reach New York from Boston. The refugees, many of whom traveled by foot, took several.

Encounters in the Wild

Depending on the plans of the Judge and the tastes of the players involved, this section of the adventure can go by in the blink of an eye or can be drawn out to constitute its majority. The roads themselves are in relatively good condition all the way into Connecticut, and the route is, of

course, passable as the party is simple retracing the path that the refugees took to reach the colony. Beyond that it is anyone's guess. Once they deviate to enter another city to scavenge what they can, the party may very well be faced with washed-out bridges, destroyed highways and buried road. The roads are not the only concern however, even before that point there are a multitude of misfortunes that may (or may not) befall the characters.

Torrential Rains

Despite the surprisingly cold weather and light snow of the morning as the team left Boston, the weather takes a radical turn. Warming up significantly, the light snow becomes drizzle. The clouds in the sky continue to darken and the rain intensifies until it becomes a downpour, a deluge the likes of which the characters have not seen in quite a while. Visibility is soon reduced to zero, and even before that wise drivers will slow the trucks to avoid skidding along the road. The characters certainly cannot defeat a rainstorm, they can simply wait it out and hope that they are not at the base of a muddy hill. After all, a mud slide or flash flood could damage their vehicles beyond repair, if not killing them all outright. Refer to pages the Book of Numbers in ***The End***, specifically pages 249-255, for detailed rules for vehicles.

Deer Crossing

Cruising along a refreshing well-preserved stretch of road, several large animals suddenly burst from the forest that has crept to the very edge of the pavement. Success on a very difficult driving check (DC 20) is required to avoid hitting the few deer running across the road as just the wrong moment. Failure results in a collision, which requires another roll (DC 20) to remain on the road and prevent the car from running off into the woods and striking a tree, something almost guaranteed to severely damage the truck. Failing the first roll, however, results only in shocked characters and a mangled hood unless it is botched (player fails roll by more than 15), in which case repairs may be in order, at the Judge's discretion. At the very least, the windshield will be damaged or cracked, if not entirely ruined.

Technical Difficulties

Machines are far from completely reliable in the world abandoned by God. Just as the characters seem to have recovered from any previous problems and are making good time, one of their vehicles gives out. The extent of the problem is left to the Judge's needs for the story. A blown tire and a moment taken to change it is enough to reinforce the realities of travel while malfunctioning engine components may force more difficult choices. The characters may take the remaining vehicle on a detour into a nearby town, if there is one, in an attempt to find a suitable replacement—assuming they have the technical knowledge required, of course. Should the Judge need to extend the duration of the trip for whatever reason, mechanical failure is a convenient and omnipresent tool with which to do so. The Judge should make repair DCs appropriate to his or her needs.

Familiar Companions

After a while, it becomes clear that the characters are not alone in their travels. Observant characters, or those familiar with the wilderness (Wilderness Skill or Spot checks at DC 17), will notice that a group of bikers can be seen a good distance behind them every now and then, apparently following them. This suspicion is confirmed if the characters double back, as the bikers will continue past them as if nothing was out of the ordinary, refusing any calls to stop and talk. A short time later, as the party continues along its way, the bikers can be spotted again, still following them a respectable distance behind.

If the characters ever do pass by the bikers or come close to them in any other manner, they will realize that they carry the same strong and unmistakable scent of blood as the Mastiffs. Further heightening the paranoia, after catching sight of the bikers three or four times, extremely observant characters (Spot DC 25)) will actually see one of the Mastiffs watching their tiny caravan from a rocky outcropping overlooking the highway. Another member of the pack pads through the forest behind it.

Man Against Nature

Most of **Act III** deals with the theme of "Man Against Nature" as the characters struggle against the elements and the wilds through their journey. This is intended to serve a dual purpose of providing an alternative to more human and finite antagonists as well as an opportunity to showcase the way the world has changed after the Rapture. Nature, as has been mentioned, is not an opponent to be *defeated* so much as *endured*, unlike more familiar adversaries such as another warrior or survivor. A journey into the wilderness of New England puts the players face to face with the fact that man has lost his dominion over the animals of the world and things are profoundly different now.

December is not the kindest of months in New England. It is cold and harsh even in the modern era, let alone after God's departure. Temperatures often drop below freezing during the day and are almost always so after dark. Warm clothing, such as coats, hats and mittens, are essential to avoid simply freezing to death during the coldest times. A fire is the easiest way to ward off this cold, but is not portable and can attract unwanted attention. If the characters are really fortunate, the heaters within the trucks will still work, providing them safe and reliable warmth as long as they function. If they fail, they can be repaired (minimum DC 20 given the cold, experience should be awarded).

Keeping a close track of food and fuel is of vital importance if the Judge wants to lend an air of danger or tension to the story, especially if delays and mishaps extend the duration. The party has enough supplies to last them several days, perhaps even a week if they tightly ration it. If misfortune robs them of part of that or forces them to travel for much longer than that, they will need to forage for food, either in a surrounding town or hunt in the wilderness itself. Depending on their competence at either task, that need may lead to a host of further complications.

And, of course, it is important to not forget that the very wilderness the characters are traveling through harbors mysteries and horrors the likes of which man has not known for centuries or more. They could just as easily stumble across something best left undisturbed as discover a supply cache they seek, though the DC should be extremely high (at least 25+).

The Surprise in the Heart of Hartford

The mysterious bikers take no direct action against the characters unless attacked, however, and eventually the party reaches the city of Hartford in the heart of Connecticut, assuming they manage to prevail against the trials of Mother Nature and do not turn back. True to hopes, it has been left largely unmolested. The Blues has caused more direct damage than any looting. Scavenging is relatively easy (DC 10), turning up plentiful amounts of canned food and even much-needed medical supplies. Furthermore, fuel is easily recovered, if the characters also search around for suitable receptacles. Armament and appropriate ammunition is somewhat more difficult to come by, as the gun shops were among the first to be looted. Nothing spectacular can be found, but standard rifles and handguns and more typical bullets than the characters would know what to do with are left.

Persistent searching across the city will eventually reveal the true prize in Hartford, however. Searching further afield, beyond the edge of the

THE END

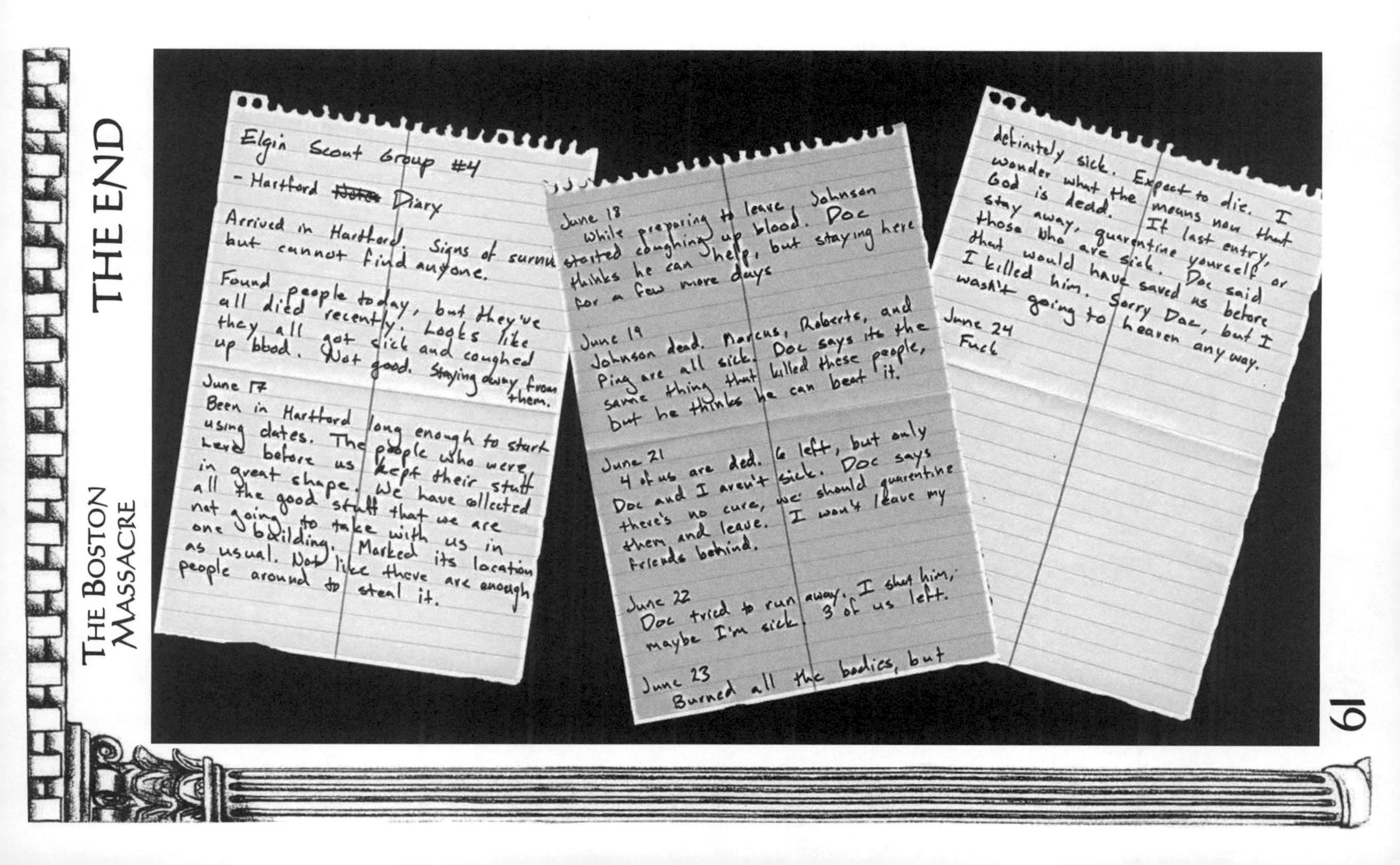

Elgin Scout Group #4

- Hartford ~~Notes~~ Diary

Arrived in Hartford. Signs of surviv but cannot find anyone.

Found people today, but they've all died recently. Looks like they all got sick and coughed up blood. Not good. Staying away from them.

June 17
Been in Hartford long enough to start using dates. The people who were here before us kept their stuff in great shape. We have collected all the good stuff that we are not going to take with us in one building. Marked its location as usual. Not like there are enough people around to steal it.

June 18
While preparing to leave, Johnson started coughing up blood. Doc thinks he can help, but staying here for a few more days

June 19
Johnson dead. Marcus, Roberts, and Ping are all sick. Doc says its the same thing that killed these people, but he thinks he can beat it.

June 21
4 of us are ded. 6 left, but only Doc and I aren't sick. Doc says there's no cure, we should quarentine them and leave. I won't leave my friends behind.

June 22
Doc tried to run away. I shot him, maybe I'm sick. 3 of us left.

June 23
Burned all the bodies, but definitely sick. Expect to die. I wonder what the means now that God is dead. If last entry, stay away, quarentine yourself or those who are sick. Doc said that would have saved us before I killed him. Sorry Doc, but I wasn't going to heaven anyway.

June 24
Fuck

city, characters stumble across large arrows painted in the roads, pointing deeper into Hartford. Very obviously left after the Rapture, many characters may be very suspicious of wherever they may lead. Following the trail of arrows, however, will simply bring them to a courthouse. As far as anyone can tell, it is abandoned, and entering will confirm that as the case. The building is far from empty, however (Search, DC 15).

A wide variety of stores, from foodstuffs to medical supplies to weaponry, has been gathered and neatly arranged within, stores away from windows and the elements. Depending on the party's success scavenging before, what they find here may be superior to their own products. Perhaps more important than these supplies, however, is a journal of sorts. On a table outside of the store room (Spot DC 25, Search DC 17) that the characters may very well miss when they first enter the building, is a short document, apparently from whoever left this cache of supplies.

From the story on the paper, a traveler from another colony to the west, in Elgin, created this depot. Sparse on the details of that colony, the document does say that the depot was established for the use of other other visitors from Elgin, should they follow. It says that some of the residents of Elgin were attempting to find colonies around them, hoping to establish ties with other survivors. The document is dated in June, almost six months ago.

A Hidden Enemy Revealed

Remaining somewhat quiet and aloof during the journey, the three refugee guides, Thaddeus O'Malley (See Appendix C), Jennifer Geffer (Standard Refugee), and Svetlana Lakteina, (Standard Refugee) never the less do their best to ensure the success of the mission. In fact, they seem zealously dedicated to it. They may leap into dangerous situations ahead of the players or volunteer to scout ahead alone. Additionally, should the characters all lack the necessary wilderness survival or mechanical repair skills necessary to keep the story moving, the refugee guides can step in to fulfill whatever roles are needed. They conceal a second and much more dangerous surprise, however.

When they had left Boston, one of their refugee companions had evidenced the faintest hint of a cough DC 30). By the time the party has reached Hartford and finished their search of the city, all three are constantly wracked with fits of coughing, often of blood. If mishaps and delays have drawn the trip out, their symptoms will become more and more evident before they manage to make it to the city. It takes about two days for the disease to run its course and for the coughing and fatigue to be undeniable, at which point they are too infirm to assist in scavenging or foraging or even any activity. It is obvious that the refugees are infected with whatever disease killed Keith Lyons and Roberta Kaplan.

How the characters deal with this dilemma may vary widely. Hard-hearted ones may very well abandon their comrades on the side of the road at the first sign of illness, desperate to avoid infection. More compassionate characters will likely make some attempt to help, perhaps searching for helpful medical supplies or trying to provide some comfort at least. Characters with Medical- Treat Illness and other medical skills may attempt to aid them normally. If the characters succeed, award experience, but the guides will suffer a relapse and die quickly the next day.

If they do offer to help, Thaddeus O'Malley will ask the characters to look for a few herbs and plants, none of which mean anything to characters not versed in holistic medicine, and then proceed to grind them into a gritty paste and chew upon the mixture. Sharing the mixture with his fellows, it very obviously relieves their suffering to a much greater extent then any of the Doctor Dahlke's treatments were able to. It is, however, not a cure, and the refugees all die by the next morning, choking on their own blood. Extraordinarily skillful medical attention may extend their suffering until the afternoon, but death is inevitable, and they are aware of that.

If pressed on how he knew about the treatment that he used to ease the pain, Thaddeus O'Malley will be noncommittal at first, dismissing the question with some half-hearted comment about knowing some alternative medicine. A Sense Motive check (DC 10) will reveal this to be false, however. In the face of further questioning, Thaddeus O'Malley will reveal that during the trip from New York, the refugees had watched the disease claim some of their own. The first victim, Jennifer Paige, fell ill almost immediately after leaving and two others followed her soon after. Thaddeus O'Malley, tears in his eyes, will recount how Jennifer had this same mixture prepared as she was dying to ease her pain. It did not allow her, or the others who had been infected, to survive long enough to reach Boston, however. The other refugees buried them along the way.

If asked why the refugees had told the colony nothing of this, or if the characters accuse Thaddeus O'Malley that he and the other refugees have brought a deadly disease into Boston and may well have condemned nearly a thousand people to death, he will begin to weep openly. The refugees had told themselves that they were not infected, that the disease has passed over them, when they got to Boston. Desperately clinging to the idea that everything would be okay once they reached their destination, they kept silent about the disease. Obviously they were wrong.

Characters can, and may very well be likely to, continue interrogating and berating Thaddeus O'Malley. Even with his treatment, however, he and the other refugees continue to worsen. None of them know a cure for the disease, nor do any have even the slightest clue as to its origin, other than its sudden appearance after they left New York City. All a burdened with guilt and remorse, even though it does nothing to bring back those who may have already fallen to the disease back in Boston. Eventually the futility of further questioning should become apparent to the characters and they will be faced with the decision of what to do with the refugees, both before and after their deaths.

ACT IV: THE BOSTON MASSACRE

The Mastiffs of War

As the characters leave Hartford, they face the Mastiffs again almost immediately. Instead of the rather aloof encounters they have had before, however, this time the Mastiffs are much more direct and aggressive. The entire pack, all four massive beasts, stands in the middle of the road north. The characters will have to take an alternate path or attempt to barrel through the creatures. If they do attempt to turn and take a different route, they manage to get a short distance further before turning a bend to see the Mastiffs waiting for them again, arrayed across the street and blocking passage.

If the characters attempt to run the Mastiffs over, they will dodge and jump onto the pickup truck and begin savagely attacking anyone they can reach. If everyone is within the cab of each truck, the Mastiffs will try to break the rear window, which only takes them a few moments considering their bulk and viciousness. Characters can attempt to shoot or throw the Mastiffs off the vehicles, and the driver can attempt to throw them free as well, although that is difficult and dangerous. Throwing the Mastiffs off requires a Grapple check for struggling characters, and the driver may make a Driving Skill check (DC 15). Success knocks one Mastiff off. Failure on the drive roll simply leaves the Mastiff on the truck, but a failure by more than 10 could cause supplies to be damaged or lost, or even run the truck off the road at the Judge's discretion. Throughout the enter conflict, the stench of old blood is almost unbearably strong.

The Mastiffs of War fight until they are killed or left behind. They give no quarter and fight as viciously as, well, animals.

Mood and Theme – A Race Against Time

Returning to a more action-packed and tense atmosphere, like that of **Act II**, this final chapter in this story is one of a race to avert tragedy, or at least attempt to minimize it. The characters have managed to establish the connection between the refugees and the disease they brought with them to Boston. Instead of the relatively leisurely pace of the previous act, this one has a much more ominous deadline. The characters must return to Boston and alert the colony to the danger, hopefully in time to halt the spread of the disease as much as possible. If nothing else, the treatment that Thaddeus O'Malley has shown the characters can ease suffering and perhaps even slow the disease as a cure is researched.

On top of this are whatever supplies the party may have managed to gather, perhaps including the information about the Elgin colony. If Boston wants to make use of this and attempt to strike up some sort of alliance with Elgin, Jefferson will have to move fast before a harsh winter makes such long-distance travel even more dangerous.

Time is of the essence.

THE END

Just What Are the Mastuffs of War Anyway?

The Mastiffs of War play a very mysterious role in this adventure. They show up at important moment, look ominous and threatening, and then leave. They almost seem omnipresent. Many players will naturally want some sort of resolution or explanation for these supernatural beasts, but as they are one of the mysteries leading to the truth about Washington, D.C., the Mastiffs of War are left unexplained at this point.

From the Mastiffs' actions and abilities, it is clear that they are not natural. Characters may get hints about their true nature from their actions, as they often lead the army or presage some sort of attack. Additionally, if the characters manage to kill on of them and have the opportunity to examine a body, they may find out more. The Mastiffs do resemble mastiffs close up, though they are larger and more muscular. There is also a disconcerting reddish tint to their teeth and claws, which are wickedly curved and serrated, making them even more menacing. Their eyes are also tinted red, though it is not obvious until they are closely examined.

Judges who want to insert some sort of resolution are free to do so, but may find it a difficult without introducing entirely new characters solely for the purpose of explaining the Mastiffs to the players. Alternatively, a Judge could provide more information about the Mastiffs without completely explaining them, especially if he or she intends to continue their campaign and eventually involve Washington. If the Judge does not intend to continue the adventure beyond the events here, it is advisable to come up with some sort of explanation about the Mastiffs to provide to curious players.

Pale Riders

However the characters manage to free themselves of the Mastiffs, their troubles are far from over. Not long after they have left the beasts behind them, a Spot check (DC 8) will reveal that four more Mastiffs (no matter how many the characters managed to kill previously) are again passively watching the party from another rocky outcropping overlooking the highway. They make no move to assault the group again.

A short distance down the road, however, the bikers return, coming up behind the party and advancing fast. Attempting to chase them down, the bikers will accelerate to dangerous speeds, shooting at the characters when they can. In order to not be quickly overtaken will require a difficult Driving check (DC 20) and losing the bikers is a nearly impossible roll (DC 25). Without extreme luck or some sort of plan, the characters will have to eventually face the bikers, of which there are 2 for each of characters.

Just like the Mastiffs, the bikers will hound the party until destroyed. Unlike their canine counterparts, however, they will not reappear once vanquished. When destroyed they remain so.

Should the characters manage to survive this encounter and kill a biker (or take a bike) they will find the new orders the bikers have recieved (below).

The Orders

From Command, Washington: Verification BZ3445

The Plague is in Boston. Pull back from and do not engage the city. Mission parameters are containment. Search and destroy any parties leaving or entering Boston. Retrieve plague victim, full quarantine procedures.

Tough Choices

Even should the characters manage to overcome the Mastiffs and the bikers, they have not resolved everything. The most important conflict is in Boston itself. Barring any extreme delays during their journey, the party is the first of the four to return. They are met warmly by their fellow colonists, if somewhat guardedly. During their absence, at least four more people have died from the disease and ten other, including 5 refugees, have shown that they are infected. Jefferson and his Sons of Liberty are beginning to fear the worst. Fear is rampant, and morale is low.

If the characters managed to return with any supplies, they are quickly unloaded and distributed. Depending on the group's success, they should be of significant help to the colony. Furthermore, if they were able to discover the evidence leading to the Elgin colony far to the west, Jefferson is very excited, speaking of organizing an ambassadorial mission to ask for aid. It is, however, the information regarding the disease and its connection to the refugees that is of the greatest magnitude.

If the players have managed to make the connection, and share it with Jefferson, he is outraged, as is the entirety of Boston. The colony feels hurt and betrayed by the people it welcomed with open arms, and perhaps rightly so. This resentment will quickly develop into anger before Jefferson is able to move to stop it. Cries of

Arguments

There are a number of arguments that the players may use in an attempt to sway the decision regarding the refugees towards mercy. None of these really apply should they advocate the exile of the refugees, however. The council will be easy to convince of the wisdom in that course of action.

Appealing to some sense of mercy or pity is unlikely to get very far, unless the characters are particularly eloquent and moving. The council hopes to rid itself of a deadly disease for which is has no cure along with the refugees. The fact that those refugees hid the existence of their affliction from the colony goes a long way to destroying any good will they may have otherwise received.

Arguing the logical point that simply excising the infected (refugees and colonists) from the body of Boston may not stop anything will have better luck, but is also unlikely to succeed. Even though other members of the colony could already be infected, exiling the refugees as punishment or simply revenge for their deception is a hard thing to dissuade most councilors from.

Sadly, perhaps the most successful tactic would be to appeal to the Sons' of Liberty attempts to uphold the old American ideals of freedom, equality and democracy. Accusing the councilors of putting the needs of the many before the few or oppressing the minority may shame them into mercy, as would claiming that they are using the ends to justify their means, thus cheapening the "American Dream."

Particularly cruel Judges may want to have someone bring up the possibility of the refugees, after being exiles, simply turning around and joining forces with Washington, bargaining their knowledge of the colony and its defenses for survival. In this case, the choice changes from exile to *execution*. Judges should also be aware that some bloodthirsty players may suggest the same thing.

THE END

vengance rise, but cooler heads prevail and Jefferson quickly calls for a meeting of the heads of the colony, putting a trusted guard around the remaining refugees and disease victims, both to protect them and to restrain them in isolation. The only one allowed out is Nancy Kassell (Standard Refugee, except +4 CHA), who has taken the leadership role in the group after Rebecca Richards fell ill. She is taken to address Jefferson's council. Alternatively, players could both role- and roll-play this confrontation using Diplomacy, Intimidate, Bluff, and Sense Motive skills. The Judge will have to decide the difficulty of these checks as the scenario plays out, but we suggest

reasonable easy DC's and an experience award for the players (but only if they intervene).

Boston is faced with really only two options. The colony can either expel the group of refugees or not. If they are given mercy and not expelled outright from the colony, it must be further decided whether to segregate them or not, as well as determining whether or not they should be held accountable for their transgressions, perceived or real. Simply expelling them, on the other hand, is a much clearly choice. No further qualifications need to be made.

Virtually everyone on the council initially calls for expulsion, although Jefferson is the one to initially bring up allowing the refugees to stay. Nancy Kassell argues bitterly against exile, pointing out that with deep winter approaching and a hostile army to the south, that is simply a death sentence and a cruel one at that. This is where the characters can perhaps make their biggest contribution to the colony's future, one way or another. They have the chance to attempt to sway the decision one way or another, as they desire. The Judge should award a CR 10 equivalent experience bonus if the party can avoid a massacre or brutal exile.

Should the characters have failed to determine the link between the disease and the refugees, Jaime Dahlke will realize it within a week, but not after more than twenty victims succumb. Then the same issue will be laid before Jefferson and his council, but this time the characters will have significantly less influence. Instead it will be the doctor, advocating the expulsion the infected in hopes of saving those still healthy, who has the greatest influence.

Mercy Rules

Even if they manage to prevent the outright exile of the refugees, the characters are unlikely to have been able to do it without some sort of compromise.

A quarantine of all infected colony members, whether they were originally refugees or not, is assumed, but there are likely to be other stipulations. Perhaps they had to make political deals in order to gather the support they needed to secure the victims' safety. Any questionable deals or shady alliances they had to make will now likely come due, perhaps with dire consequences.

As a result of their passionate defense of the refugees, they may be given the responsibility of finding a cure for the disease. "If you want to ensure the survival of the refugees, then it is your responsibility to ensure the survival of the colony itself." The search for a possible treatment or cure could grow into an entirely new campaign as the characters travel across the new world, perhaps even to the diseas's creator, Pestilence himself.

Furthermore, even if the Council does decide to spare the refugees exile or execution, the mere fact that they considered it and came so close to doing so will create a massive amount of resentment on both sides. Tensions will run high and tempers will often flare up. Perhaps more dangerously, any sort of quarantine program must be carefully managed, or Nancy Kassell and the rest of the refugees may grow to feel like they have indeed been exiled in all but name. The characters, as defenders of the refugees, will likely be called upon to mediate any disputes and keep relations cool until the disease has been eradicated, if that is even possible.

Out Into the Cold

Without impassioned and convincing reasoning, the council will decide to expel the refugees, turning them out into the cold with minimal supplies. Lots to determine those responsible for expelling the refugees are drawn up and distributed among the able-bodied soldiers in Boston. All of the player characters draw the short sticks, forming the core of the force. If they did not protect the refugees, they will be forced to do the colony's dirty work, executing the will of the council.

The refugees, for their party, will obviously resist this. Lead by Nancy Kassell, they refuse to be marched off to what they see simply as their deaths without a fight. Still possessing not only their own weaponry, but also what was provided to them during the fighting, the refugees will resist to the last. Holed up inside the very building that the characters lead them to at the very start of the story, Boston will be forced to fire upon them if the colony intends to stand by its decision.

Unless the characters manage intervene at the last minute to change things, this will ultimately culminate in a massacre as Boston slaughters the refugees. Mediation without combat should earn the players *more* experience than combat, but will be understandably difficult. The Council has made its decision and is loathe to rescind it. In fact, the refugees' promises to fight back only harden many of the councilors' resolve. Nancy Kassell and her refugees are acutely aware that they will be marched off to their deaths if they give in, they simply cannot survive alone. Kassell knows how unlikely it is that the Council will change its decree, but she cannot see any other choice. Either her people die alone out in the cold or here, fighting back against their murderers. It will be nearly impossible to convince them to surrender.

Unfortunately for Boston, not every refugee sees the situation as that hopeless, and a handful will attempt to escape. Most will travel north or east, but some will head straight for the invading force to the south, hoping to trade information for shelter and safety. That would be disastrous for Boston, and it will be the character's responsibility to ensure that none of them escape alive.

Epilogue and Resolution

After the massacre is averted or cleaned up, Boston has further problems it must face within the next few months, perhaps immediately. Depending on their actions during the preceding events, they may have similar roles to play in these further plot threads, should the Judge explore them. Characters who aggressively took central positions during the adventure and proved themselves capable of the responsibility will further their standing in the colony and can exert great influence over the future of the colony. Alternatively, they could be sent to look for a cure.

Judges looking to continue the story of Boston and its desperate residents have a number of large plot threads with which they can weave the foundation of further stories, with or without any other published adventures. Each will, of course, require work to fully flesh out into a working adventure, but all can be expounded upon and expanded to fit most any group of Meek in ***The End***. Appendix A has further suggestions and advice as well.

The Refugees

If they were not destroyed by the Boston colony, or if some fled during the last stand, the refugees will undoubtedly figure prominently in the colony's future. If they were spared and allowed to remain part of the colony, even if isolated for health concerns, they are incredibly grateful and

loyal to Jefferson. Their devotion sometimes exceeding even that of older Boston residents, some may develop a sort of martyr complex and their bravery and sacrifice against the invaders reach new heights. Alternatively, perhaps they hold to key to curing the deadly disease the entire colony faces, even if they do not know it themselves. If one refugee recovers from the illness Jaime Dahlke might be able to fabricate an inoculation or even a cure.

The Disease

With or without the refugees that brought it, the disease that some residents have begun to call Lyons' Plague remains an immediate and deadly foe. During their journey to Connecticut, the characters had a chance to learn a temporary treatment for the effects of the plague. A compassionate Judge might allow them to develop a better treatment or even a full cure from it. Perhaps in the wilds changed by the Rapture there is some antidote they can seek out, or perhaps the Rapture has changed diseases as well as animals and this plague is not what it had seemed at first. Regardless, without some treatment and cure, the plague will continue to ravage Boston, slowly killing its residents. By spring, Washington will have no one left to fight. Alternatively, the adventure could end the discovery of a poultice which occasionally cures the disease. It may even be revealed by an agent of the Horsemen Pestilence who realizes that completely wiping out the refugees will prevent his creation from spreading...

Washington, D.C.

The Sons of Liberty will still have to face War, even should they manage to defeat the plague. Whatever supplies or assistance the other scouting teams manage to return with is left to the Judge's imagination, but without a miracle Boston will emerge from the harsh winter weakened and barely able to slow down the stronger Washington's advance, let alone stop it or push it back. A miracle could take many forms. A quick and easy cure for the disease could be one. A timely alliance with another strong colony could be another.

Elgin

If the colony can resolve the disease, Elgin stands as their key to survival. It is clear that the invaders are the stronger force by far, and though Boston does not lack courage or determination, it does desperately need reinforcements, something that the events of this adventure have only exacerbated. If Jefferson can enter into an alliance with the Elgin colony and heavily draw upon them for assistance, he might not only be able to keep his precious colony alive, but finally defeat the army that has been harrying his city. At least until Washington, DC decides to send another invasion force.

APPENDIX A

JUDGE'S ADVICE

The Boston Massacre is an adventure designed to accomplish a number of things. As mentioned in the **Introduction**, the ultimate intent of the story was to put the characters in the middle of a very difficult decision, a choice between two evils. Do they force a group of people they have come to care for out to their deaths or allow them to stay and condemning virtually everyone they know to death? Is it acceptable to sacrifice a few in an attempt to save many? That is not the only goal of the adventure, however. It also sought to allow the characters a chance to become deeply involved in the politics of Boston, reveal the nature of their enemy and to provide the colony with the hope of establishing alliances with other settlements. It is important to keep these central threads in mind when dealing with possible complications or problems as well as enacting alterations to the material presented, as all Judges are sure to do. Make sure characters act in a manner which reflects the world they live in and their Sin.

Possible Complications

There are a number of possible complications that potential Judges should be aware of, both when they

are planning their sessions and when they are running them. Trying to keep these central elements in mind at all times can help avoid insurmountable obstacles further down the road in the adventure. Neglecting one can not only lead the adventure into areas unanticipated by this material, but, more importantly, they can cause nonsensical plot developments or pitfalls. If the players never associate with the refugees and have never left the Boston colony, then the entirety of **Act III** becomes almost impossible to explain. Judges should try to maintain a solid grasp on the story and, when necessary, taking some time to draw out the adventure in places to ensure that required events or revelations come to pass.

At the same time, however, avoiding simply railroading the players is an important concern. While the Judge may feel that a certain scene is of vital importance to the story, the players will become extremely frustrated if they feel like their decisions don't matter. This is, in part, why *The Boston Massacre* is presented as such a skeletal adventure. The essential events are described and it remains up to the Judge to flesh them out in such a way as to give the players' decisions the influence they deserve.

A Link Between the Players and the Refugees

A lot of the details of this adventure rely upon the assumption that the refugees and the characters share some sort of close interaction, that they were the first ones to find them and welcome them into the colony. It is this assumed relationship that leads to the characters' roles in traveling with the three refugee guides in the journey detailed in **Act III**. Even more importantly, without either some degree of emotional investment the ultimate dilemma of the adventure looses much of its impact. If the characters do not view the refugees as their friends and allies, it will become much easier for them to decide that expelling them from the colony is the correct course of action.

Judges should make an effort to ensure that such a relationship develops. Provide the character with the opportunity to interact with the refugees and get to know them well. The first and second acts provide ample opportunity for this. Mixed patrol groups in the first act have plenty of time to talk with each other and become acquainted with each other while attempting to determine the full extent of the invasion force. In **Act II**, daring refugees may come to the characters' rescue, or simply fight alongside them valiantly. Alternatively, the refugees can be used to provide something for more noble characters to protect; victims in need of saviors. Players looking for noble quests or characters motivated primarily by compassion may respond well to that.

The Connection Between the Disease and the Refugees

Another possible source of friction for the smooth development of the plot in the adventure is the connection between the plague and the refugees. It can be very easy for players to miss it entirely if their characters aren't in the right places at the right times. If the characters are not involved in the expedition in **Act III** or they do not persuade Thaddeus O'Malley to talk with them, providing the evidence they need to confirm any suspicions they may already have, the events of **Act IV** are changed significantly. Without the sense of urgency to

THE END

return to Boston and attempt to avert the continued spreading of the plague, the characters are likely to take much longer scavenging in Hartford, returning in high spirits in expectation of a hero's welcome. What they will find, however, is only more people already infected by the disease, and many more will succumb and die before someone else makes the connection, thus precipitating the confrontation of **Act IV**. Providing the characters that did not attempt to draw the truth from Thaddeus O'Malley before his death with a guilty journal that also reveals everything can be a way to salvage **Act IV** without too many changes, even if it may seem a bit strained.

Similarly, if the characters are given the impression that the refugees intentionally brought the disease into Boston, deciding upon exile will be very easy. While the refugees were deceitful in that they did not warn the colony that they had suffered losses from disease on their journey, they were desperate and had attempted to convince themselves the danger was past. They were not intent on killing anyone, they just wanted safety and shelter and prayed that everything would be all right once they reached their destination. Tragically, they were wrong and their self-delusion could very well destroy their haven.

At the same time, however, it is also important to make sure that the players don't stumble across the truth too quickly. If they make the leap and figure everything out in **Acts I** or **II**, they will find the rest of the colony rather skeptical of their claims until more and more people start dying. The first visible victim of the disease is a colonist and not a refugee for precisely the purpose of concealing that link for as long as possible. Later the players stumble across a victim who died before Keith Lyons, but it shouldn't be until **Act III**, when the characters are far from Boston, that the realization dawns. Without that realization, the need to return to Boston in time to avert an epidemic, and the sense of accomplishment and closure doing so can provide, simply is not there. Judges should try to balance rewarding players for their insight against the greater needs of the story, perhaps adding red herrings and potentially misleading evidence to create a sense of doubt.

Washington, D.C., as the Home of the Invasion Force

While not having a significant impact on the events within this book, making the nature of the invasion force clear is of central importance for the future stories that *The Boston Massacre* is only the first installment of the Chronicles of WAR or another campaign. This is, perhaps, the easiest one to address as well, for Judges have a wealth of sources that they can use to provide their players with information about the army threatening Boston.

The equipment that the soldiers use is one very simple device, as Washington, D.C. license plates or police equipment will make the ultimate source of the army clear to most players. The invaders are using converted Washington Police Department vehicles and riot gear, many of which retain distinguishing features such as logos or initials. Additionally, captured prisoners or even defectors could provide confirmation of their origin, talking about Washington. It is recommended, however, that the Judge keeps the details vague at this stage. Washington, D.C. is a mysterious and ominous threat on the East Coast that none of the other colonies have reliable or solid information on. It is a dangerous unknown. The easiest way to accomplish this is to limit captured or talkative soldiers to conscripts and volunteers from New York or the areas under Washington dominance, who have not gone to the city themselves and discovered whatever truth may be there.

The Mastiffs of War, and the rag-tag bikers, are also connected to Washington, D.C., and that may be a much harder link to reinforce. If they feel that their players have not made the connection, Judges may want to add in more appearances by the Mastiffs, having them run just in front of invading troops or moving through the columns of soldiers marching in the streets. The soldiers are not connected with the Black Spike Gang noted in The End. Similar devices used to associate the invaders with Washington can be used here as well. While it is unlikely that one of zealous and belligerent bikers will be restrained and interrogated, they can be depicted as using Washington equipment as well, and are likely to have district license plates on their bikes as well. Presenting both the invaders and the Mastiffs of War as clear and present enemies should form a connection between the two in the minds of most players, but Judges should still keep this element in mind.

Altering the story

Every Judge is going to run their own, unique version of the tale outlined here, such is the very nature of role playing. Many, however, will dramatically depart from the ideas here, working in their own ideas for further plot developments or involving the elements of ***The End*** that they and their players most enjoy. A

Judge who wants to highlight the hope of the Meek rebuilding a society after God has left will likely create a much more optimistic ending to *The Boston Massacre*. Another who loves the supernatural atmosphere of the game will work in the strange and unexplained throughout the game. There are a number of dimensions that the adventure can be easily expanded into, and ambitious Judges should take them under consideration.

Deepening

Many gaming groups like very detailed role-playing experiences, with a greater emphasis on communication and character interaction than on combat or physical conflict. Others, however, do not. This adventure attempts to accommodate both, the ultimate conflict and drama of the story is very much a social and moral one, but there are ample opportunities for bloodshed and thrilling action.

Judges hoping to encourage more role-playing and character development may find the introduction of more social events very helpful. Boston is, after all, a community of people before anything else, and will have feasts, holidays, parties and funeral services. Patrols provide a somewhat tense and anxious opportunity for in-character interaction, as does a tense standoff between opposing forces. Those are not the only choices, however. Jefferson holds open councils most of the time, and colony members are encouraged to involve themselves in Boston politics. Despite being at war, the people must still go about their lives and they eat and involve themselves in various forms of recreation, from reading to swimming to dancing to sex. The arrival of the refugees sees much of the colony coming out to greet the strangers, at least until the invaders attack, and they are robbed of that luxury. Judges may want to role play through the Thanksgiving celebrations that take place before the refugees arrive if they want to ensure that the players are very familiar with the major NPCs of the city. Funerals for colonists who fell during the fighting are another social venue in which the players can interact with a number of NPCs, as well as serving to reinforce the tragic nature of life in ***The End***.

One the other hand, many Judges will look to increase opportunities for combat and action in the story, and each act can easily accommodate that. **Act II** is the most combat oriented of the four and the few days of the major Washington advance can easily be drawn out into several sessions worth of running battles and desperate assaults, even without making the conflict last longer within the game itself. **Act I** and **Act III** provide the most opportunities for fights between small groups to break out, as the characters are patrolling their city for the enemy in the first and exploring uncharted wilderness in the second.

Expanding the scope

The scope of this adventure is relatively small and confined. The characters can have a great impact on the future of Boston, but they do not save it outright, nor does their failure immediately damn it either. Beyond that, the events described here are all within a few days' travel of each other. This is not a country-spanning epic, but that may not appeal to some groups. Scope can be expanded with a little additional work, however.

Only the effect of Lyons' Plague on Boston is presented in this adventure. Broadening the disease's range to threaten other colonies can provide a much more epic opponent to struggle against. In this case, it becomes necessary for the characters to have some effective means of combating it, however. As previously mentioned, the treatment that Thaddeus O'Malley showed to them may allow the players to develop a cure or they may endeavor to go on a grand quest to discover one. Once they have it, their work has just begun as they tour the nation to distribute it and save as many lives as they can. Through this nomadic story, they are faced with a number of different conflicts and may hold the fate of entire cities in their hands as well as the questions that responsibility creates. If the characters are opposed to slavery, for example, do they provide the cure to Atlanta?

Freeing Boston from the danger of invasion is another epic story line, but a somewhat more difficult one. Without a miracle or a whole lot more people, the colony would find defeating Washington, D.C. once and for all impossible. The invasion force threatening them directly, however, may be more easily conquered. Judges may want to reduce the size of the invading army or allow the characters to lead the colony forth into battle with amazingly successful strategies to vanquish their enemies. This, however, runs the danger of removing much of the danger from the story.

Adding in other Horsemen

Probably one of the most common and enticing changes would be to directly involve the Horsemen in the events of Boston. Doing so unavoidably emphasizes the occult and supernatural feeling of ***The End***, but that may very well be the desired result. The story already involves a great deal of fighting and disease, as well as a concern for food supplies and death, so the domains of all of the Horsemen are already woven in. Further use of the Horsemen could involve the inclusion of their direct minions or just symbols of their influence, depending on whether the Judge wants to paint them as active forces or more abstract and transcendental beings.

War is already deeply involved in Boston, through its conflict with Washington, and this is an idea that will be further developed upon in later adventures and chronicles. Indeed, the Mastiffs of War are not frivolously named. War clearly has a stake in the area, and an agenda he is trying to fulfill. Further emphasizing his involvement is most easily accomplished by increasing the appearances of the Mastiffs, as well as their more supernatural aspects. Turning the canine Mastiffs into spiritual dogs or monsters and the bikers into avatars of War would make almost any player feel the influence of the Horseman.

Pestilence is the other easiest Horsemen to bring more directly into the conflict, through the disease that forms the center of the story. Lyons' Plague may very well be a personal creation of Pestilence. Perhaps it is a spiritual servant of the Horseman, infecting one host before moving on to another, maybe even allowing the characters to use magical means to directly defeat it. Judges seeking to avoid the moral complications of the story or looking for a more conspiratorial feel may turn the refugees from innocent victims to willing servants of Pestilence. Insane worshippers of a dark god, they have come to infect the colony and kill in the name of their infectious lord. Are they immune to their own diseases? Why does Pestilence want to spread those diseases? Does he claim the souls of those who die from them? If so, to what purpose is he gathering such power? A proliferation or rats or the appearance of other disease can be used to provide a more abstract feeling of Pestilence's presence.

With the colony's concern about having the food necessary to survive the winter, the influence of Famine can be felt, but only lightly. A plague of flies or other insects, exceedingly rare in winter, can serve as a symbol of the Horseman's presence, but a more direct interest could take the form of food stores mysteriously disappearing or rotting. Famine may be directly responsible for this himself, or he may employ saboteurs or cultists of his own.

Finally, Death is ever popular and nearly omnipresent Horsemen. Often seen as the most aloof, enhancing his influence could be as simple as having a murder of crows roosting above every death scene or as complicated as introducing a "pale rider upon a pale horse." Whether a traditional image of the reaper making his way through the carnage atop of stallion or something as modern as the trench-coat wearing biker riding through the chaos, Death may be one of the most powerful and frightening Horsemen for most players. Judges can play on that fear and use Death as a holy terror to humble the characters or play against it with Death taking a much more pleasant tone.

Symbolism

A concentrated effort to include symbolism within the game can be used to accomplish any number of effects. Within the adventure as presented, symbolism is used extensively. The Mastiffs of War, for example, not only symbolize the presence of the Horseman War in the story, but mark the changing of the acts as well. Including other Horsemen in the game will likely involve other symbolic representations or animals. The Horsemen are far from the only things that the Judge may want to use in a symbolic manner. Foreshadowing is often accomplished through symbolism, as is a story's meaning. Entirely different themes and messages can be introduced through innovative implementation of symbolism. Anything from the weather to colors to sounds to smells to simple numbers (4 Horsemen, 4 Mastiffs, 4 Acts) can be used to provide hints to what is going on behind the scenes in a story, reinforce some message or to simply engender an atmosphere of the surreal.

APPENDIX B:

FOUNDER

REBORN (PRESTIGE) CLASS

The Founder prestige class is only open to those intrepid Meek who have decided to build a community in a particular location in the dangerous world of The End. These individuals have been forged by the experience of being left behind into resolute leaders who seek to preserve the old ways and restore mankind to its glory... one brick at a time.

Hit Die: d2

Prerequisites:

Base Attack Bonus +2.

Diplomacy 3 ranks, Knowledge (Geographic Area) 3 ranks.

Must be founder of colony. A colony for this purpose consists of more than 10 people living in a fixed area for at least one month.

Class Skills:

Bluff (Cha), Construction(Wis), Diplomacy (Cha), Gather Information (Cha), Knowledge (Area) (Int), Innuendo (Wis), Intimidate (Cha), Mechanical(Int), Perform (Cha), Ridicule (Int), Scavenge (Area Only) (Wis), Sense Motive (Wis), Spot (Wis).

Skill Points:

3 plus Int Modifier per level

Armor and Weapon Proficiencies:

None

Special Abilities:

Inspire: Founders may Inspire as Preacher by making a stirring speech.

Greater Inspire: As Preacher.

Blues Resistance: Blues Resistance is the most powerful aspect of the Founder Prestige class. Due to their close connection to humanity and its creations as well as the Founder's goal to to rebuild vestiges of those creations, the Founders and those items they interact resist the influences of the Blues. Blues Resistance (Personal) prevents any item on the Founder's person from suffering from the Blues and provides a +2 bonus on any check to see if an item breaks or fails. Blues Resistance (Location) prevents the home or headquarters of the Founder (and anything contained in it) from suffering from the Blues (up to a 60' radius). Blues Resistance (Create Icon) is the most powerful Founder ability in that it allows a Founder to cause an item or building to become an Icon and develop a permanent resistance to the Blues. Icon creation costs a minimum of 1,000 experience points for every square foot an item takes up in volume. The Founder must also spend one day in the presence of (within 60') the item per 10,000 experience points expended. These days must be spent consecutively.

Founder Level Table

Level:	Base Att Bonus	Fort	Ref	Will	Special
1	+0	+0	+0	+1	Inspire 1/day
2	+0	+1	+1	+2	Inspire 2/day
3	+1	+2	+1	+2	Gain Leadership Feat
4	+1	+2	+2	+3	Gain Dodge Feat
5	+2	+3	+2	+3	Blues Resistance (Personal)
6	+2	+3	+3	+4	Uncanny Dodge (Area Only), Inspire 3/day
7	+3	+4	+3	+4	Greater Inspire 1/day
8	+3	+4	+4	+5	Blues Resistance (Location)
9	+3/+1	+5	+4	+5	Greater Inspire 2/day
10	+3/+1	+5	+5	+6	Blues Resistance (Create Icon)
11	+3/+2	+6	+5	+6	Greater Inspire 3/day
12	+3/+2	+6	+6	+7	Uncanny Dodge

Uncanny Dodge (Area): Within the Area of his colony, the Founder gains the extraordinary ability to react to danger before his senses would normally allow him or her to do so. She retains her dexterity bonus to Armor Class, cannot be flanked, and gains a +2 bonus to reflex saves.

Uncanny Dodge: As Uncanny Dodge(Area), but the Founder has this ability regardless of where he or she is.

APPENDIX C:

NON-PLAYER CHARACTERS AND CREATURES

MASTIFFS OF WAR

Hit Dice: 3d10 (28 hit points)
Initiative: +4 (Dex)
Speed: 30 ft.
Armor Class: 16 (+4 Dex) (+2 Natural)
Attacks: Bite +7 melee
Damage: 1d6+3
Face/Reach: 5 ft.
Special Attacks: None
Special Qualities: Frightful Presence, Scent

Saves:	Fort +6, Ref +8, Will +3
Abilities:	Str 16, Dex 17, Con 15, Int 7, Wis 14, Cha 10
Skills:	Hide +9, Listen +6, Move Silently +7 Spot +9
Feats:	Alertness
Climate/Terrain:	Any
Organization:	Pack 2-4, 5-20
Challenge Rating:	3
Treasure:	None
Advancement:	None

Frightful Presence: As the tools of the Second Horsemen of the Apocalypse (War), the Mastiffs radiate an unsettling presence and the scent of blood. Humans within 30 feet who have less than 30 hit points may become *frightened* or *shaken* (See pg 84-85 DMG) if they fail a Will Save (DC 15). Humans who succeed at the save are immune to its effects for one day.

Scent: The Mastiffs may detect opponents within 30 feet by sense of smell. If the opponent is upwind, the range increases to 60 feet; if downwind, it drops to 15 feet. When a creature detects a scent, the exact location is not revealed-only its presence within range. The creature may take a partial action to note the direction of a scent, and if it moves within five feet of a scent, it may pinpoint the scent's location. A creature with scent may follow tracks by smell, making a Wisdom check (typically DC 10 modified as appropriate) to follow or find a track. In addition, the Mastiffs receive a +1 racial Bonus to Listen, Move Silently, Hide and Spot checks. The Mastiffs also receive a +2 bonus to Wilderness Lore checks when tracking by scent.

SONS OF LIBERTY SOLDIER ("SOL")

Sin: Varies
Place of Birth: Varies
Apparent Age: Varies
Citizenship: Boston
Type/Class/Level: Meek 4
Challenge Rating: 4
Size: M
Hit Dice/Points: 27 Hit Points
Initiative: +6 (+2 Dex, +6 Improved Initiative)
Speed: 30 ft.
Armor Class: 13 (Armor +1, Dex +2)
Attacks: +3
Saves: Fort +1, Ref +1, Will +4
Abilities: Str 13 (+1), Dex 15 (+2), Con 15 (+2), Int 10 (+0), Wis 10 (+0),Cha 12 (+1)

Skills: Climb +3, Bluff +2, Disguise +3, Driving (Automobile/ Motorcycle) +4, Gather Information +3, Heal +4, Hide +6, Jump +2, Wilderness +3
Feats: Improved Initiative, Firearms-Pistol, Rifle, Shotgun, Any three of the following: Blind-fight, Combat Reflexes, Endurance, Firearms Proficiency- Military, Iron Will, Lightning Reflexes, Toughness
Special Abilities: Survivor, Soul
Possessions: At a minimum, the equivalent of a Kevlar Vest (Good), one firearm (Good), unlimited ammunition, and other general equipment. Judge should adjust to fit the encounter.

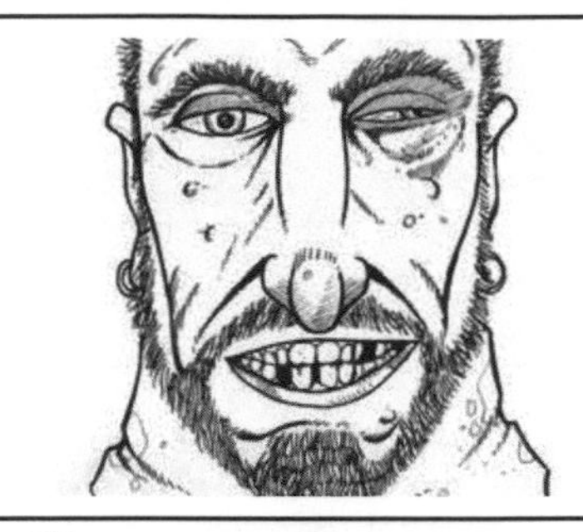

TYPICAL REFUGEE ("REFUSE")

Sin: Varies
Place of Birth: New York or varies
Apparent Age: Varies
Citizenship: New York
Type/Class/Level: Meek 2
Challenge Rating: 2
Size: M
Hit Dice/Points: 12 Hit Points
Initiative: +0
Speed: 30 ft.
Armor Class: 10
Attacks: +1 or +2
Saves: Fort, Ref, Will
Abilities: Str 9 (-1), Dex 11 (+0), Con 10 (+0), Int 11 (+0), Wis 11 (+0), Cha 10 (+0)

Skills: Climb +2, Bluff +2, Disguise +1, Driving (Automobile/ Motorcycle) +2, Gather Information +1, Heal +2, Hide +3, Jump +2, Knowledge (New York) Wilderness +3. These can be adjusted to reflect particular Professions or crafts as well.
Feats: Any 3 of the following- Alertness, Combat Reflexes, Endurance, Iron Will, Lightning Reflexes, Toughness
Special Abilities: Survivor, Soul
Possessions: Minimal. Most items in Worn or Damaged Condition. Very few firearms (nothing superior to a hunting rifle), plus clubs, knives, staves.

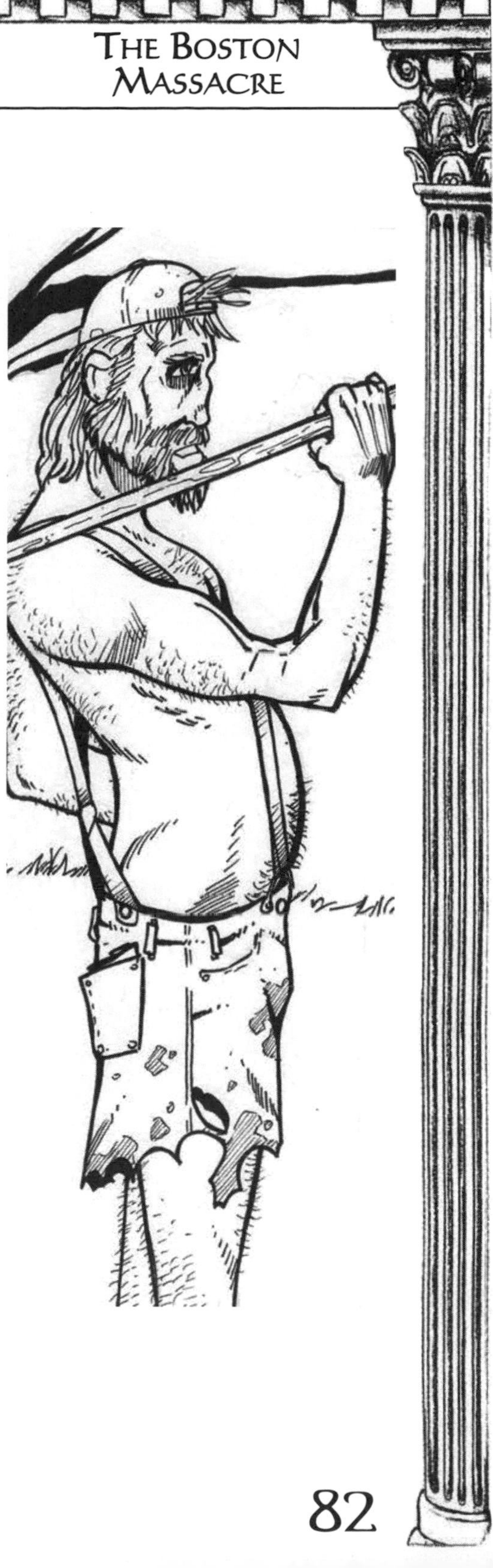

TYPICAL MEMBER OF THE BIKER ARMY ("RAG TAG")

Sin: Varies
Place of Birth: Varies
Apparent Age: Varies
Citizenship: Washington, D.C.
Type/Class/Level: Meek 3
Challenge Rating: 3
Size: M
Hit Dice/Points: 20 Hit Points
Initiative: +1 (Dex)
Speed: 30 ft.
Armor Class: 12 (+1 Armor, +1 Dex)
Attacks: +2
Saves: Fort +1, Ref +1, Will +3
Abilities: Str 13 (+1), Dex 12 (+1), Con 13 (+1), Int 10 (+0), Wis 10 (+0), Cha 12 (+1)

Skills: Climb +3, Bluff +2, Disguise +3, Driving (Automobile/ Motorcycle) +4, Gather Information +3, Hide +5, Jump +3, Wilderness +3
Feats: Firearms Proficiency- Pistol, Rifle, Shotgun; Any three of the following: Blind-fight, Combat Reflexes, Endurance, Iron Will, Lightning Reflexes, Toughness
Special Abilities: Survivor, Soul
Possessions: At a minimum, the equivalent of a Kevlar Vest(Worn), one firearm (Good), and other general equipment. Judge should adjust to fit the encounter.

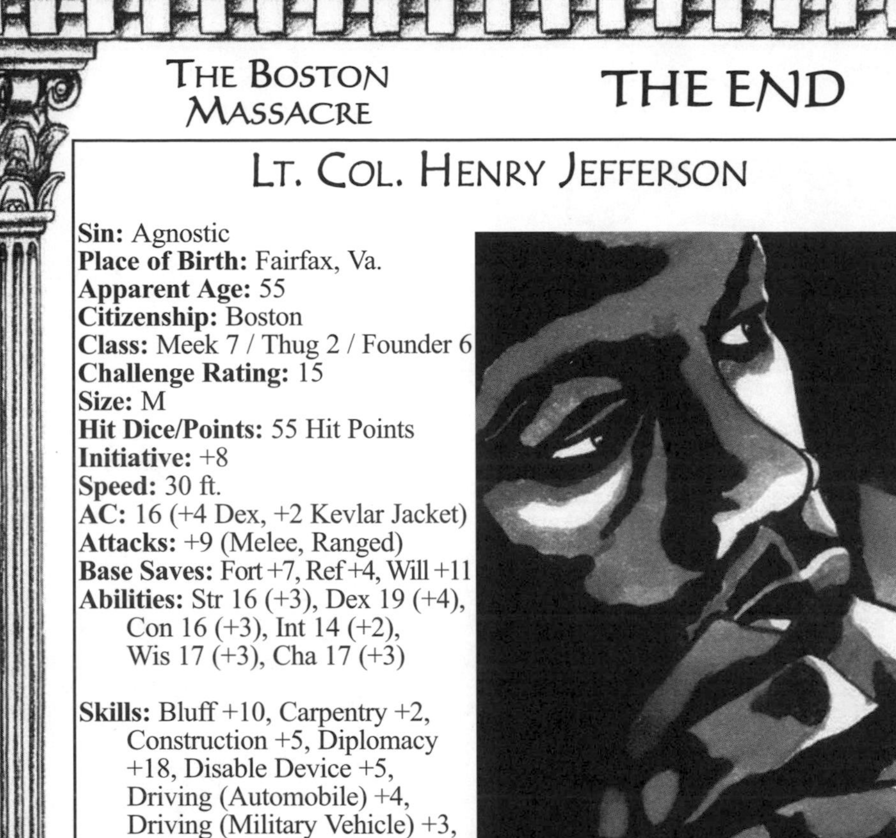

LT. COL. HENRY JEFFERSON

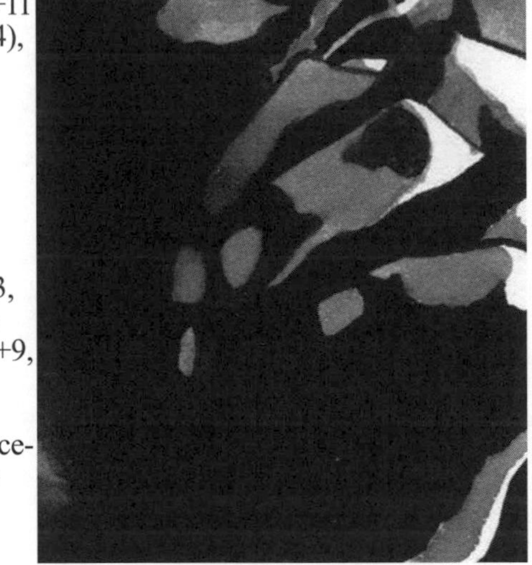

Sin: Agnostic
Place of Birth: Fairfax, Va.
Apparent Age: 55
Citizenship: Boston
Class: Meek 7 / Thug 2 / Founder 6
Challenge Rating: 15
Size: M
Hit Dice/Points: 55 Hit Points
Initiative: +8
Speed: 30 ft.
AC: 16 (+4 Dex, +2 Kevlar Jacket)
Attacks: +9 (Melee, Ranged)
Base Saves: Fort +7, Ref +4, Will +11
Abilities: Str 16 (+3), Dex 19 (+4), Con 16 (+3), Int 14 (+2), Wis 17 (+3), Cha 17 (+3)

Skills: Bluff +10, Carpentry +2, Construction +5, Diplomacy +18, Disable Device +5, Driving (Automobile) +4, Driving (Military Vehicle) +3, Gather Information +3, Hide +5, Innuendo +5, Intimidate +9, Knowledge (Boston) +7, Mechanical +2, Perform +5, Science- Electrical +4, Science- Chemistry +5, Sense Motive +5, Spot +2, Tumble +2, Wilderness +2

Feats: Alertness, Automatic Weapon Proficiency, Expertise, Firearms Proficiency - Military, Improved Critical (Desert Eagle), Mobility, Point Blank Shot, Power Attack,Precise Shot, Quick Draw, Rapid Shot, Stabilize, Weapon Specialization (Desert Eagle) (THG), Endurance (THG), Leadership (Fou), Dodge (Fou)

Special Abilities: Survivor, Soul, Inspire 3/day, Blues Resistance, Uncanny Dodge (Area Only).

Possessions: Kevlar Jacket (Ex), FN-FAL Rifle (Ex), Desert Eagle (Good), 6grenades (Ex) and unlimited ammunition.

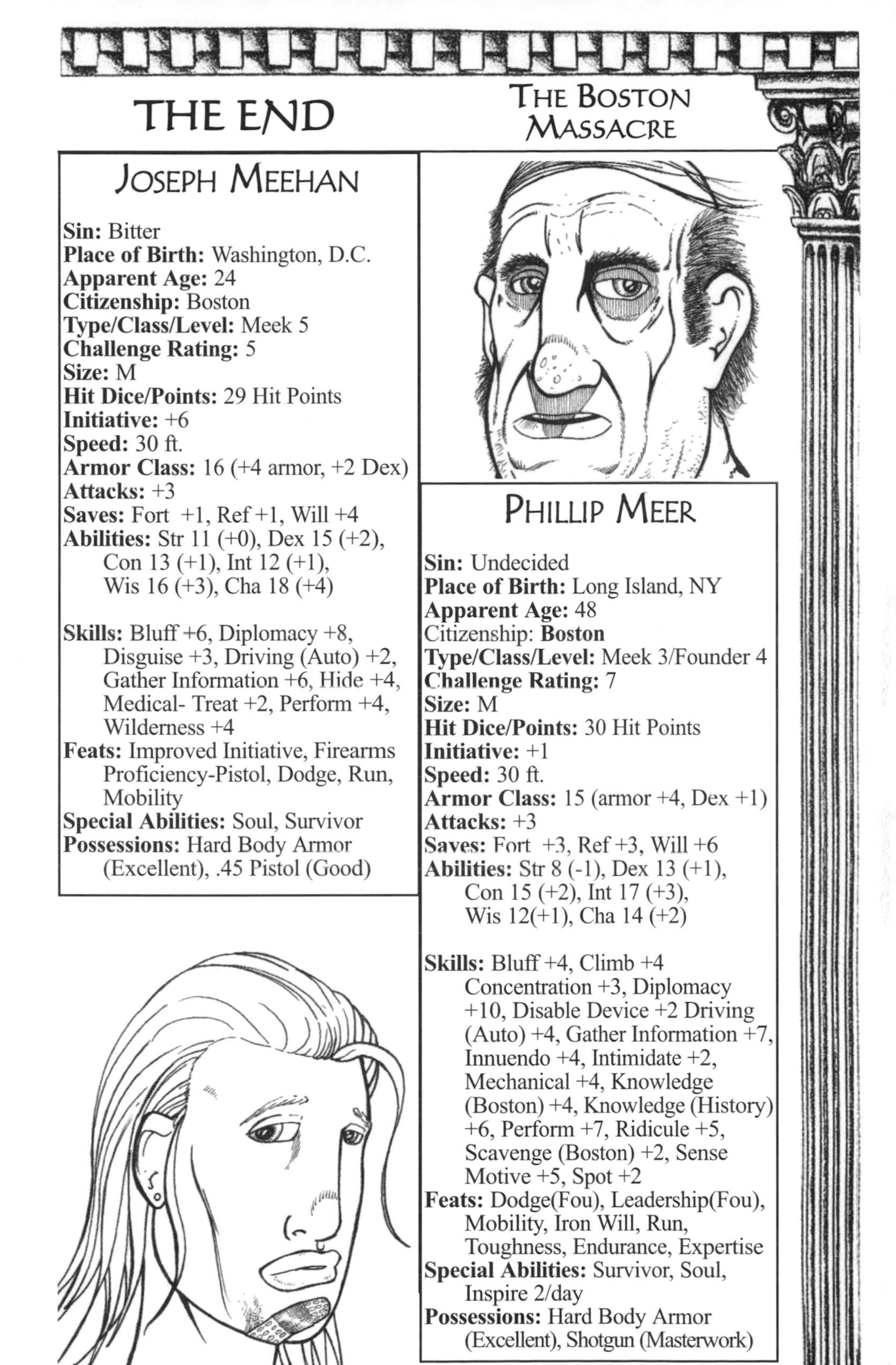

JOSEPH MEEHAN

Sin: Bitter
Place of Birth: Washington, D.C.
Apparent Age: 24
Citizenship: Boston
Type/Class/Level: Meek 5
Challenge Rating: 5
Size: M
Hit Dice/Points: 29 Hit Points
Initiative: +6
Speed: 30 ft.
Armor Class: 16 (+4 armor, +2 Dex)
Attacks: +3
Saves: Fort +1, Ref +1, Will +4
Abilities: Str 11 (+0), Dex 15 (+2), Con 13 (+1), Int 12 (+1), Wis 16 (+3), Cha 18 (+4)

Skills: Bluff +6, Diplomacy +8, Disguise +3, Driving (Auto) +2, Gather Information +6, Hide +4, Medical- Treat +2, Perform +4, Wilderness +4
Feats: Improved Initiative, Firearms Proficiency-Pistol, Dodge, Run, Mobility
Special Abilities: Soul, Survivor
Possessions: Hard Body Armor (Excellent), .45 Pistol (Good)

PHILLIP MEER

Sin: Undecided
Place of Birth: Long Island, NY
Apparent Age: 48
Citizenship: **Boston**
Type/Class/Level: Meek 3/Founder 4
Challenge Rating: 7
Size: M
Hit Dice/Points: 30 Hit Points
Initiative: +1
Speed: 30 ft.
Armor Class: 15 (armor +4, Dex +1)
Attacks: +3
Saves: Fort +3, Ref +3, Will +6
Abilities: Str 8 (-1), Dex 13 (+1), Con 15 (+2), Int 17 (+3), Wis 12(+1), Cha 14 (+2)

Skills: Bluff +4, Climb +4 Concentration +3, Diplomacy +10, Disable Device +2 Driving (Auto) +4, Gather Information +7, Innuendo +4, Intimidate +2, Mechanical +4, Knowledge (Boston) +4, Knowledge (History) +6, Perform +7, Ridicule +5, Scavenge (Boston) +2, Sense Motive +5, Spot +2
Feats: Dodge(Fou), Leadership(Fou), Mobility, Iron Will, Run, Toughness, Endurance, Expertise
Special Abilities: Survivor, Soul, Inspire 2/day
Possessions: Hard Body Armor (Excellent), Shotgun (Masterwork)

The End

Jamie Dahlke

Sin: Humanist
Place of Birth: Des Moines, IA
Apparent Age: 33
Citizenship: Boston
Class/Level: Meek 4/Physician 3
Challenge Rating: 7
Size: M
Hit Dice/Points: 20 Hit Points
Initiative: +4
Speed: 30 ft.
Armor Class: 16 (+2 Armor, +4 Dex)
Attacks: +4
Saves: Fort +5, Ref +2, Will +8
Abilities: Str 12 (+1), Dex 18 (+4), Con 10 (+0), Int 17 (+3), Wis 13 (+1), Cha 14 (+2)

Skills: Animal Empathy +3, Bluff +1, Climb +2, Concentration +4, Diplomacy +2, Driving (Auto) +3, Medical-Treat Illness +7, Medical Investigation +5, Medical-Treat Wounds +7, Professional (Doctor) +3, Read Lips +3, Spot +5, Science-Chemistry +6, Science-Electric +3, Wilderness +2
Feats: Improved Initiative, Dodge, Mobility, Stabilize, Run, Combat Medic 1, Counter Poison 1, Improved Treatment 1
Special Abilities: Soul, Survivor, Nature Sense
Possessions: Medicine Kit and Tools (Excellent)(pretty much every thing a combat doctor could carry), Kevlar Jacket(Good), Knife(Good), Glock .22 (Good)

Susan Cominsky

Sin: Agnostic
Place of Birth: Boston, MA
Apparent Age: 25
Citizenship: Boston
Type/Class/Level: Meek 6
Challenge Rating: 6
Size: M
Hit Dice/Points: 31 Hit Points
Initiative: +2
Speed: 30 ft.
Armor Class: 12
Attacks: +4
Saves: Fort +2, Ref +2, Will +5
Abilities: Str 7 (-2), Dex 15 (+2), Con 15 (+2), Int 14 (+2), Wis 11(+0), Cha 16 (+3)

Skills: Animal Empathy +2, Balance +2, Climb +4, Disguise +2, Handle Animal +7, Intuit Direction +5, Jump +4, Language/Literacy +1, Medical-Treat Wounds +3, Ride +7, Spot +3, Swim +1, Wilderness +8
Feats: Alertness, Firearms-Rifle, Dodge, Point Blank Shot, Stabilize, Track
Special Abilities: Soul, Survivor
Possessions: Horse (Excellent), Saddle (Excellent), Rifle (Good), Sword (Good)

Rebecca Richards

Sin: Polyglot
Place of Birth: New York, NY
Apparent Age: 63
Citizenship: New York
Type/Class/Level: Meek 3/Founder 3
Challenge Rating: 6
Size: M
Hit Dice/Points: 21 Hit Points
Initiative: +0
Speed: 30 ft.
Armor Class: 10
Attacks: +3
Saves: Fort +3, Ref +2, Will +5
Abilities: Str 6 (-2), Dex 10 (+0), Con 12 (+1), Int 14 (+2), Wis 17 (+3), Cha 15 (+2)

Skills: Bluff +5, Diplomacy +7, Hide +4, Knowledge(New York) +7, Language/Literacy +2, Medical-Treat Illness +3, Medical-Treat Wounds +4, Perform +5, Sense Motive +3, Spot +2
Feats: Leadership (Fou), Alertness, Endurance, Iron Will, Stabilize
Special Abilities: Soul, Survivor, Inspire 2/day
Possessions: Staff (Good), Basic First Aid Kit (Good), Glock .22 (Good), 2 clips worth of ammunition (Good).

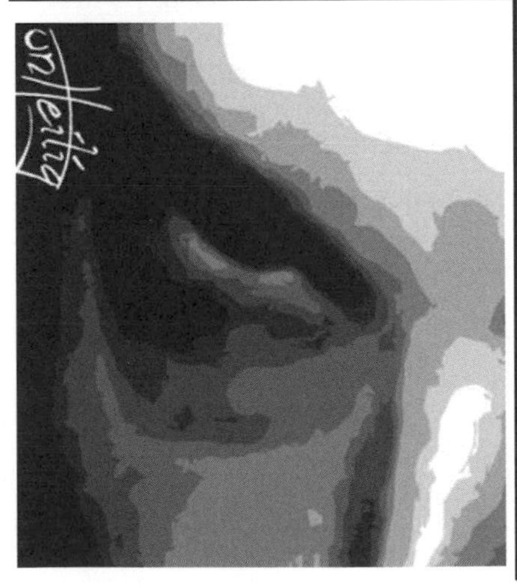

Thaddeus O'Malley

Sin: Sinner
Place of Birth: Dublin, Eire
Apparent Age: 36
Citizenship: New York
Type/Class/Level: Meek 4/Digger 2
Challenge Rating: 6
Size: M
Hit Dice/Points: 21 Hit Points
Initiative: +6 (+2 Wariness, +4 Dex)
Speed: 30 ft.
Armor Class: +4 (Dex)
Attacks: +4 (+5 Submachinegun)
Saves: Fort +2, Ref +3, Will +5
Abilities: Str 10 (+0), Dex 18 (+4), Con 17 (+3), Int 14 (+2), Wis 14 (+2), Cha 15 (+2)

Skills: Bluff +5, Carpentry +3, Climb +4, Disable Device +5, Drive (Automobile) +4, Intuit Direction +4, Knowledge (Boston) +5, Mechanical +5, Move Silently +2, Search +3, , Scavenge +5
Feats: Alertness, Combat Reflexes, Expertise, Firearms-Military, Weapon Focus (Submachine Gun)
Special Abilities: Soul, Survivor, Dig Down, Pack Rat, Wariness
Possessions: Kevlar Jacket(Good), HK MP-5 SubmachineGun (Excellent), Glock .22 (Good)

The End

Walton Norfleet

Sin: Sinner
Place of Birth: Omaha
Apparent Age: 50
Citizenship: Washington, D.C.
Type/Class/Level: Meek 7/Thug 4
Challenge Rating: 11
Size: M
Hit Dice/Points: 48 Hit Points
Initiative: +6 (+2 Dex, +4 Improved Initiative Feat)
Speed: 30 ft.
Armor Class: 16 (+4 Armor, +2 Dex)
Attacks: +9 (+2 Dmg with Pistol)
Saves: Fort +3, Ref+6, Will +6
Abilities: Str 16 (+3), Dex 15 (+2), Con 16 (+3), Int 14 (+2), Wis 9 (-1) , Cha 15 (+2)

Skills: Balance +4, Bluff +8, Climb +3, Diplomacy +2, Driving (Automobile) +5, Gather Information +10, Intimidate +10, Jump +5, Move Silently +3, Perform +7, Spot +13, Wilderness +6

Feats: Automatic Weapon Proficiency, Combat Reflexes, Firearms Proficiency-Pistol, Firearms Proficiency-Shotgun, Improved Critical (Colt .45 Pistol), Improved Initiative, Leadership, Point Blank Shot, Weapon Specialization (Colt. 45 Pistol) (THG), Endurance (THG)

Special Abilities: Soul, Survivor

Possessions: Hard Body Armor (Good), Colt .45 Pistol (Good), FN-FAL Rifle (Good), 6 Frag Grenades (Good)

Richard Patel

Sin: Sinner
Place of Birth: Boston, MA
Apparent Age: 30
Citizenship: Boston
Type/Class/Level: Meek 5
Challenge Rating: 5
Size: M
Hit Dice/Points: 30 Hit Points
Initiative: +1
Speed: 30 ft.
Armor Class: 15 (+4 Armor, +1 Dex)
Attacks: +3
Saves: Fort +1, Ref +1, Will +4
Abilities: Str 15 (+2), Dex 12 (+1), Con 17 (+3), Int 10 (+0), Wis 10 (+0), Cha 10 (+0)

Skills: Climb +6, Driving(Auto) +6, Hide +6, Intuit Direction +4, Listen +4, Spot +6
Feats: Alertness, Firearms Proficiency-Rifle, Firearms Proficiency-Military, Toughness, Track
Special Abilities: Soul, Survivor
Possessions: Hard Body Armor (Good), M-16 Rifle (Good)

DAVID TARR

Sin: Bitter
Place of Birth: Boston, MA
Apparent Age: 40
Citizenship: Boston
Type/Class/Level: Meek 3/Founder 4
Challenge Rating: 7
Size: M
Hit Dice/Points: 26 Hit Points
Initiative: -1
Speed: 30 ft.
Armor Class: 14 (Armor +5, Dex –1)
Attacks: +3
Saves: Fort +3, Ref +3, Will +6
Abilities: Str 10 (+0), Dex 8 (-1), Con 15 (+2), Int 12 (+1), Wis 16 (+3), Cha 16 (+3)

Skills: Bluff +5, Diplomacy +9, Driving (Auto) +3, Forgery +2, Gather Information +2, Hide +2, Innuendo +5, Intimidate +2, Knowledge (Boston) +5, Perform +4, Profession (Business) +5, Ridicule +5, Wilderness +1
Feats: Leadership (Fou), Dodge (Fou), Alertness, Body Armor Proficiency, Great Fortitude, Point Blank Shot
Special Abilities: Soul, Survivor, Inspire 2/day
Possessions: Hard Body Armor (Good), Megaphone (Worn), Ruger MP9 (Good)

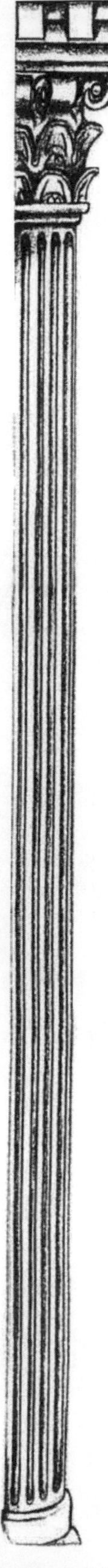

FIRST PRINTING © 2002 Tyranny Games;
"The End" under license from Joseph Donka

Tyranny Games LLC
804 Robertson St
Wauwatosa, WI 53213
United States
www.tyrannygames.com

Printed in the USA.

4. Breach and Cure
In the event that You fail to comply with the terms of this License, You will be considered to be in breach of this License. Wizards of the Coast will attempt to notify you in writing by sending a Registered Letter to the address listed on the most recent Confirmation Card on file, if any. You will have 30 days from the date the notice (the "cure period") to cure the breach to the satisfaction of Wizards of the Coast. If no Confirmation Card is on file, you will be considered to be in breach of this License immediately.

5. Termination
If, at the end of the cure period, the breach is not cured, Wizards of the Coast may terminate this License without further written notice to You.

6. Effects of Termination
Upon termination, You shall immediately stop all use of the Licensed Articles and will destroy any inventory or marketing material in Your possession bearing the D20 System Trademark logos. You will remove any use of the D20 System Trademark logos from your advertising, web site, letterhead, or any other use. You must instruct any company or individual that You are or become aware of who is in possession of any materials distributed by You bearing the D20 System Trademark logos to destroy those materials. You will solely bear any costs related to carrying out this term of the License.

7. Penalty for Failure to Comply with Termination Instructions
If You fail to comply with the Effects of Termination, Wizards of the Coast may, at its option, pursue litigation, for which You shall be responsible for all legal costs, against You to the full extent of the law for breach of contract, copyright and trademark infringement, damages and any other remedy available.

8. Updates
Wizards of the Coast may issue updates and/or new releases of the D20 System Trademark logos without prior notice. You will, at the earliest possible opportunity, update all material distributed by You to use the updated and/or new version of the D20 System Trademark logos. You may continue to distribute any pre-existing material that bears an older version of the D20 System Trademark logo.

9. Changes to Terms of the License
Wizards of the Coast may issue updates and/or revisions to this License without prior notice. You will, at the earliest possible opportunity, conform in all respects to the updated or revised terms of this License. For a period of 90 days You may continue to distribute any pre-existing material that complies with a previous version of the License. Thereafter written consent should be obtained from Wizards of the Coast. Subsequent versions of this License will bear a different version number.

10. Updates of Licensee information
You may transmit an updated version of the "card.pdf" Confirmation Card at any time to Wizards of the Coast.

11. Notices to Licensor:

Wizards of the Coast
D20 System License Dept.
PO Box 707
Renton, WA 98057-0707

12. No maintenance or support
Wizards of the Coast shall have no obligation whatsoever to provide You with any kind of maintenance or support in relation to the D20 System Trademark logos.

13. No Warranty / Disclaimer
THE D20 SYSTEM TRADEMARK LOGO FILES ARE MADE AVAILABLE ON AN "AS IS" BASIS. WIZARDS OF THE COAST DOES NOT MAKE ANY REPRESENTATION OR WARRANTY, WHETHER EXPRESS OR IMPLIED, AS TO THE FITNESS FOR A PARTICULAR PURPOSE, USE OR MERCHANTABILITY. WIZARDS OF THE COAST MAKES NO REPRESENTATION OR WARRANTY THAT THE D20 SYSTEM TRADEMARK LOGO FILES ARE ERROR-FREE.